AF254502

AMYGDALA BLUE

AMYGDALA BLUE

PAUL LOMAX

atmosphere press

© 2022 Paul Lomax

Published by Atmosphere Press

Cover design by Ronaldo Alves

No part of this book may be reproduced without permission from the author except in brief quotations and in reviews.

atmospherepress.com

TABLE OF CONTENTS

Religion

Racism

Relationships

The time
cracks into furious flower. Lifts its face
all unashamed. And sways in wicked grace.

> — Gwendolyn Brooks, "The Second Sermon
> on the Warpland," (1968)

I will keep Broken Things.
I will keep You:
Pilgrim of Sorrow
I will keep Myself

— Alice Walker, *The Cushion in the Road: Meditation and Wandering as the Whole World Awakens to Being in Harm's Way* (2013)

We are the heirs of a legacy of creative protest [...] the teachings of Thoreau are alive today, indeed, they are more alive today than ever before.

> — Dr. Martin Luther King, Jr., *Massachusetts Review,*
> Autumn (1962)

RELIGION

My Imaginary Friend

November 1963. As long as I can remember, sixty-six Books of the Bible (KJV) served as my *Father*, I was my mother's favorite *Son*, and in our home, I always had a great time playing with someone I called the *Holy Ghost*.

But in my neighborhood, life sometimes existed within a fifth dimension Rod Serling would've loved to direct as a *Twilight Zone* episode.

"Their house is so strange," is what I once believed all of my neighbors thought of us.

As a child, barely 7 years old, I was quite convinced Quebec Place was a lovely neighborhood. With its battalion of thick, cicada-infested oak trees standing guard, small, elevated manicured lawns, spring-like awnings, streamline of American made cars parked all along one side of our hilly street, Quebec Place was nestled in an upper-middle-class, multiethnic district located in the northwestern section of Washington, DC.

Its row house fabric was generationally serene, sown with a seasonal sunshine that was as timely as the mailman, cool as the milkman, refreshing as the ice cream man, and complete with over-seer neighbors who were given approval to whip your butt if you overstepped your boundaries when your parents were away at work.

In their colorful ways, everyone on our block seemed so full of directions, everyone had complete families, and everyone drank milk and honey flowing from their glasses of togetherness and devotion. But in our neighborhood, there existed some things as uneasy as sitting outside the principal's office, waiting. Within our neighborhood, everyone seemed to give sermons with their eyes that drifted like an early morning fog over a distant shoreline. Most of the adults, that is. Sermons I remember attending to on a daily basis, and from the front row whenever I passed by or came over to visit with a friend or two.

What's wrong with your mother?
Who does she think she is?
Where is your family?
Why are you so different?
We know your kind –
Know where you've been –
We know where your kind goes!

I often wondered why it was so important for adults to preach during the middle of the week when it wasn't Sunday, when there was no sign of a church or steeple in sight. Furthermore, why was there so much discussion about my household, when all around me, everyone else was just as guilty of testa-lying and speaking in forked tongues?

Our home wasn't strange. Our wardrobe wasn't comprised of fig leaves, and we weren't miserable Christians waiting next in line for the hungry lions to gnaw on our sacred flesh. No. Just because our house never held parties and I had no father, and my mother never entertained guests or there were no visitations from extended family members. Just because my mother walked about in a dignified manner, carried a bible with her wherever she went, minded her own business, and chose to tend her garden of scarlet zinnias, amaryllis, bittersweets, bluebells, and magnolias. Whereas I remember them, my neighbors, sat around like lost crows on their front porches surrounded by nasturtiums, snapdragons, begonias, yellow hyacinth, and marigolds.

Did they think our home was strange because we honored and obeyed 'rules' regarding the proper use of Standard American English and "No movie theatres or ungodly shows," or because I could only watch certain television programs my mother unapologetically called that *"one-eyed devil?"* Maybe because we did not violate commandments regarding conservative clothing and no late hours. "Be home before the streetlight comes on," I remember my mother always saying.

Maybe we were strange because my mother held her Pentecostal bible study in our house twice a week. Sometimes I began to believe them, especially during frequent sessions when I was squeezed between two oxen, 'Aunt-Esther-type' church women who always smelled like alley cats sporting 9-year-old perfume. I couldn't help but wonder, as I gathered small pockets of fresh air in between "Hallelujah!" and "Praise the Lord!" shouts, where these behemoths with their Mohammed Ali Bibles came from...

But then there remained the age-old question, *why was everyone so afraid to speak to God?* I wasn't afraid. I guess this is how I met the *Holy Ghost.* Could it have been the rhetoric of sin, damnation, and repentance that spooked my neighbors into believing we were *strange?*

I don't know. But, day in and day out, I continued to witness their whispers, picture their sideshows staged behind veiled pulpits, vague backsliding shimmering with dishonesty and deceit. Although I didn't quite understand their weeding hearts, I was able to recognize the biting sting of their words, the negative power in their Janus talk.

This is partly my reasoning in choosing the comfort of home – the stethoscope realm envisioned when *Altered States* meets *Pleasantville* – my personal coordinates to which *Star Trek's* Scotty would frequently beam me without an appreciable drain on the dilithium crystal reserve.

Within my home, the *Holy Ghost* and the walls in my room were unconditionally my friends. Upstairs, in our quaint three-bedroom home, is where I shared my deepest thoughts. The ceiling is such a long way off. It seems the light from that bulb has a long distance to travel just to touch my skin. Sometimes during the day, when time seems to slow to a commercial that never quite ends, I hear my bedroom all around me speaking in a language I've known since birth. So soft it was, reminiscent of my mother's warm milk. Although older, I was still reminded of this wondrously addictive, soothing elixir, its flavor washing down the back of my throat with water-falling knowledge. Whispers of our conversations poured still in the glass of my room, throughout the air in our house, a hush of quotidian peace tasted at room temperature.

Outside of my home, the choir of the neighborhood children playing tag, echoes of balls and bats and double-Dutch and dodgeball, swell. Crisp voices of innocence rev up for growth, car doors slam, and grocery-store bags stuffed with groceries crunch and fold, mailboxes squeak open and then cry, bicycle rubber burns against the stubborn cement, screen doors bang against front porch railings, everything surrenders to the smile of a warm day giggling against the applauding Indian summer breeze. All of this I hear calling me like the 9:00 am school bell, but instead, I chose to pay attention to the telephone still ringing in my mind, even after several hours had elapsed, reverberating with the joyous reminder: it was Thanksgiving season.

Today, mother is home. Downstairs, she busies herself about the meditation of cooking, basting and serving and poking that big, stuffed, poor, unfortunate bird. In her finest glory, she works our kitchen like an engineer peddles his locomotive engine down the world's longest track. Sometimes the windows would cake with blinding sweat, making it difficult to see outside. I wouldn't know what time of day it was, or who was watching whom. There were no clocks in our home, so I would tell time by watching people outside come and go. But I was always amazed at how trees seemed to know what was going on. Those brown-hearted saints of stature, with their branched blues which gingerly went this way, stretched that way, for squirrels to pass and fowl to perch and insects to nibble and a kingdom of leaves to sprout from. Sentinels of whispering roots, attentive to the four winds painted on the face of every day, listening to sulci grind pathways throughout endless cortical seasons. Listening to Dryads – still against the passage of time, Hamadryads against the sharpened scythe of death, Meliads against an old testament – paint over Solomon hues, speaking xylem from the coldest night, exhaling phloem blown over the warmest day. In my mind, I saw them as sentinels of whispering roots, attentive to the four winds painted upon the face of days passed.

It was this day that I remember saying to hibernating dust, meditative walls in my room: "The ceiling is such a long way off. Light from that bulb has a long distance to travel. How does dust know to hide under a chair and bed? Where are its legs? Why does Mother have to work so much? Where is my Father?"

"He is with you, always," I heard.

Up from under the chair I jumped, nearly hitting my head on the seat on the edge of the chair. In my room, a man stood before me. I didn't hear him come up our creaking staircase. I didn't hear him enter my tiny room.

He was tall, had his own light bulb which glowed around him. He seemed different, like someone I saw on the *Outer Limits* television show, hands folded in front and his face calm, not at all like my neighbors, no deeply-embedded questions and heart-choking frowns, or restless eyes dancing with sermons. I wasn't sure what to make of his feet – did they touch my wood floor? To satisfy my curiosity, I quickly bent over to look – yes, they touched the floor – then I popped back up.

"You scared me... Are you a friend of my mother?" I said.

"Yes."

"Where do you live?"

He was quiet.

"Do you know my father?"

"Yes."

"Where is he?"

"You, like many, have two fathers."

"Two...fathers?"

"Yes."

"But I only need one."

"And he is with you."

"Where?" I said, twisting my head all around my room. "He's not here!"

"Your Earthly father wasn't meant to be with you and your mother."

"Will I ever get to meet him?"

"Yes, much later in life; when you're an accomplished adult."

"Accomplished adult?"

"When you grow up and become well educated."

I stood there for a moment, trying to understand it all.

"Are you a ghost?"

"I am... your spirit guide."

"Spirit...guide?

"Yes."

"What is a spirit guide?"

"Another name for... your best friend." He paused and then continued. "Almost everybody has one like me. I happen to be more hands-on than most..."

"Like laying-of-hands for soothing in prayers?"

"Very good little one, you are quite smart. You learn well!"

"Really?" I said with a huge smile.

"Yes..."

"Do you have superpowers like the Avengers?

He was quiet again.

"Okay, I'll call you my Holy Ghost..."

As comforting as the airspace enveloping my room, my *Spirit Guide* was a Godsend. We got along just fine, and he loved to play. He knew plenty, and like a real family, was always there. He also talked with me about my neighbors, why they were so mean to me.

"Why do people think my mother is crazy?"

"Your neighbors are not wrong; they simply lack understanding. In time their hearts will understand."

"What do you mean?"

"Deep down inside, your Mother suffers."

"Suffers..."

"Yes."

"What is suffers?" I asked.

"Your mother is not well..."

"What's wrong with her? Can she go to the doctor?"

"She is in the hands of the greatest doctor."

"Why won't he heal her?"

"It's not her time."

"Time... I don't understand."

"Take my hand."

"Why?"

"To get understanding."

"Take my hand, walk this way."

"Where are we going?"

He was quiet.

"Will it help my mother get better?"

"No, but it will *prepare* you for your future...."

Because I trusted him, because I really wanted to learn what made my mother sick, I slowly lifted up my little hand and placed it into his, then he looked down at me and nodded.

The next thing I knew we had taken off, gone somewhere I had never been, so I closed my eyes.

"Where are you?"

"I'm always with you. Open your eyes."

"I'm afraid."

"Have courage little one, you are with me. Open your eyes."

When I did, I saw that my hand was still with him, and that we stood in the midst of a place unlike anything I had seen. For a moment, I thought I had walked into a *Lost in Space* episode. It was not Saturday morning, 11 am. How could this be?

"Where are we?"

"To understand all things surrounding your mother – it has been sanctioned for you to *know* your mother."

"My mother... What does sanction mean?"

"It has been agreed."

"I don't understand."

"In time you will understand."

When I looked up, we stood before my mother sitting alone in our kitchen. She did not hear us, did not see us. The base of her palm caressed the side of her darkly weathered face, her elbow plopped against the flat plane of our over-crowded kitchen table. All around her, I saw something dark, creepy like swamp water seen in the *Creature from the Black Lagoon*. I took a moment and looked over my shoulder. Suddenly, I heard oozing out from her darkness, images, voices, from another place and time...

———

Into the congregation of a stolid self, I quietly retreated. Into the crest of an unusual moment, I was taken with tears for my tithes, confusion my only offering. I wasn't quite sure what any of this was, how it had ever happened, what any of it actually meant. For the veil had lifted and behind her fractured window, I had discovered how my mother really felt about herself. To see her miserably broken from within made me want to question God. But I couldn't do such a thing as that. Did He know me? Surely He knew of mother's needs, surely He saw her cries? All of this ran over my mind like roadkill.

I wanted to seek the advice of someone close, a relative. However, there was no family member, no one I could go to for advice. I never knew or met any uncles and aunts, a grandmother or a grandfather, or any cousins, nothing of the sort. I had siblings, but my three sisters were more than twice my age, and *girls*.

"Can she be healed?"

"Your mother suffers from a diseased heart, a broken spirit."

"Momma..."

"Yes."

"Is there anything I can do to help... my... mother?" I was crying.

"Do not cry, little one. Your understanding is the beginning of a wonderful cure, and the beginning of wisdom. Your mother's suffering will be short-lived, great peace will she have, forever, and ever."

His words were foreign, moved past my little brain, but tasted like fresh cotton candy. I began to feel much better. My breathing was no longer short and heavy.

We got along just fine and like a scab from a terrible sore, all the questions, concerns, and thoughts about my mother eventually went away. Not that she had changed or was psychologically reborn again, but miraculously it just didn't matter anymore. It was no longer an issue, as I continued to love and stand by her side, providing whatever was needed or asked of me. Wash the dishes, vacuum the floor, take out the trash, paint the living room, go to the grocery store, cut the grass, sweep the porch, shovel the snow, and could you help Mrs. Taylor who lived up the street?

Moreover, the *Holy Ghost* and I continued to speak about sanguinary, existential things, and I listened, learned, and grew up trusting in the values of the older generation. It was the *Holy Ghost* who helped me understand that it was okay to not have a family and that everything in life really happens for a reason, a universal purpose. He also said when things appear horrible, they are actually a blessing in disguise; and vice versa. It was he who taught me about the price of *wisdom*, the beauty of *truth*, the wealth in *understanding*, and the value of balance and tolerance.

Words I thought would never stop jumping all over me, nudging my shoulders, crowding my personal space. However, in reality, that was not the case. For I discovered how necessary this all was, that I was simply undergoing the vital transformation of growing up and becoming a responsible man; finally beginning to understand the intricacies and verities and complications of life working things out, long after Quebec Place, the *Holy Ghost*, and I had long since departed, and my mother had gone on to be with Jesus Christ.

Requiescat in pace.

My Mother's Song

August 1967. Thursday, I'm tired.

The ground is as hard as the day is as long, hot. But I won't let this day come before the heaven that God has planned for us. No, I shall not stumble, faithless, once again sinful. My back aches from working all night, cleaning executive offices in the House Office Building on Capitol Hill, Washington, DC. I've had this job for several years. Now, I'm on my way towards the main line up Georgia Avenue to catch another bus to my second job. No one said having two jobs would be easy, certainly not a walk in the park. But, for those of color and educationally disadvantaged, this is par for the course, survival. For many of us, this is something we either do or perish – it's as plain as the Ten Commandments.

Through the grace of God, I can work. My babies will have a roof over their heads, food in the refrigerator, and heat during the winter. They will not suffer, not if there is a God. I can't think about my needs, no sir. Can't let any of those thoughts enter my mind, won't allow any of this to wreck my soul with blasphemous beliefs, ill-begotten wishes. I am a child of God, and I hear and obey your commandments, Lord. I hear and obey, Lord.

Please give me strength.

The trees lean with a lounging resonance, swaying to natural songs as pleasant and comforting as a baby's touch. No one walks the quiet, gray pavement but me. No one else must do such a thing, but me. I understand, Lord. I carry the understanding in my pores, between my legs, deep into the recesses of a cracked subconscious-ness, Lord. Just me and my Jesus walking in the rhythm of the Lord.

Walking in the rhythm of the Lord.

I like it like this, accept your ways, Lord; peaceful, meditative, spiritually liberating. I know you are watching over me Lord, guiding my every way, listening to my every thought. I know you are there – I can feel your blessed breath upon the creases of my shadow like a coat of arms. You have always been my shield and my buckler, and because of this, Lord, I shall love, honor, and cherish your words to the last of my dying breath, my last breath, Lord.

Thank you, Jesus. Thank you, Lord.

Amygdala Blue

In Bicêtre   Salpêtrière
folie à deux rage   gyri pine,—
buttocks sign   pelicans whine
i want   must have
                           Mine

Chained whispers   passed a fleet of muses
Anne: Gertrude: Silvia: Virginia:
dropping anchors along Ports of Epididymis
searching for love in garden-spun germ states
while Little Hans locked the gates
to beat Bonaparte sausage   anxiously
No mother   why must i come in
my object   has no relation

Just walk away   with your dancing uterus
dangle your stitchcraft before
grey women   crying for
Little House on the Prairie

After loving you   & you
after listening to Cerberus barking
i still wonder   am i living
conditions of Medusa hissing,—
                           moderately sad
                                       essentially mad

Symphony of Clouds

"Ouch!" she cried, pulling her dark dangling underarm husk of flab away from the blue flame.

Katherine Wright relished the meditative journey in cooking: the escape, the grandeur of a blissful introspection, the flamed intimacy she wore like a new dress. At times, it stuck in all the wrong places, sometimes it hung on her like a wet towel flung over the shower, and then there were moments when it wanted to escape.

It was an ineluctable Saturday morning, the middle of July. Frenetic birds chirped and fluttered like children splashing swimming pool water, and, glaring with an exalted attitude, the diurnal keeper pretended to mind as it stretched throughout the phlegmatic summer breeze. Through a small tear in her grease-stained shade, a slice of sun stretched like a child stealing from a candy jar.

However, there was not much in the way of candy in her distorted confectionary. There was no dishwasher, no garbage disposal, no microwave, no kitchen counter, or cutting board. No full set of dishes, the silverware was stained, glasses were unmatched, the drainer frowned with grit, one electrical outlet, and over across her tiny dimension, through the blanketed haze of a meal in progress, a picture of Jesus with 'God Bless This House' hung above their dining table. Below, a quaint dining table for two, light-brown oak with deeply engraved gashes, which spoke more to the art of ornamentation than to the issue surrounding table abuse. Over in the corner, like a displaced drunkard, an ironing board leaned against the back of the kitchen door, while lining the corners of her worn down linoleum floor were tiny decorative specs of crumbs and a cricket leg. As a fresh vegetable newly placed in the bend, in her kitchen, Katherine was home. She did not mind her loss of amenities in her kitchen. She subsisted on its airing difference. It not only fed her, spoke to her, it nurtured her. Outside of her son, Mathew, she really did not have a reason for enjoyment.

With grey hair brushed for the moment, Katherine lifted her head to catch sight of the only fly gracing the sanctity of her ointment, that greasy shade that hung over her kitchen window. She hated it, hated what it represented, and she hated what it seemed to know. As if that shade singed her reason with a judicious conviction, as if that shade halted her thought train in places she vowed never to revisit, as if that shade was an enemy, she eyed it with a cutting flame much warmer than the one she received. She despised its white, greasy, plastic, ordinariness. It was just a shade with no mean-spirited intent to do her any harm. An inanimate object that merely wanted to hang there against the inquisitiveness of the sun, to be neither too small nor too large for the window that was its task in life to cover, to be pulled this way in the evening and that way in the morning, to stir in the breezes that came before rain on a summer night, and to be much-used and little-noticed. She yanked it down.

"Mathew!" Katherine yelled, eyeballing the blue flame. "Your breakfast is ready!"

"Coming..." From upstairs, a dull thump sounded.

Trying to adjust her housedress, which hung over her like a wet sheet on a backyard clothesline, she twisted and dug, writhed in her own shadow, but nothing seemed to do. Weathered from long desolate bus stops, her graded skin tone shined like raw cowhide. After settling into her favorite chair, she shook her head, exhaled much-needed air. The fork sat in her hand, waiting, but her appetite was not there. Instead, she slapped the back of her throat with the sweet taste of a glass of cold orange juice.

"Good morning, Mom," Mathew said, bursting into the kitchen still adjusting his loosely fitted University of Pennsylvania T-shirt, shoestrings stinging the floor. "You're up early."

"I thought you'd enjoy a home-cook meal, for once," Katherine said, "Aren't you hungry?"

"Sure," Mathew said. "Something smells great."

"How are you doing at school?" Arms planted comfortably over her buxom mantel.

"Not bad," taking a seat across from Katherine, "my finals ended last week and I

think I did okay."

"What does that mean?"

"You know... not bad." The crest of his clavicle imprinted through his shirt.

"Tell me about your pre-medical courses?"

"Oh, I dropped Biochemistry. The professor was a jerk."

"Watch your mouth!"

"Mom," Mathew smiled, "the teacher was outrageous with his homework assignments. Worse, he lectured directly from the textbook. No problem, I'll take it again next semester with another professor."

He paused.

"I really enjoyed my math and p-chemistry classes, though."

Mathew was always aware of the dissimilarity between him and his beloved mother, heads double-taking, the stares whenever they went out together in the community. Growing up in Washington, D.C. was a constant reminder. He never really questioned his heritage, why no other family members called or visited, never pursued answers to questions surrounding his father's identity, his departure, the long absence, and never really tried to know what transpired between his parents twenty-one years earlier. He simply wanted to enjoy the everyday life of a struggling college student. This was all his adolescent mind could handle, cared to know.

"And your overall GPA?"

"... somewhere between 3.7 and 3.8."

Katherine listened with the attentiveness of an eagle.

Although Katherine never attended high school, barely completed junior high school, never sat before chalk-encrusted classrooms buzzing with spoiled juveniles, never experienced Greek fraternity and sorority pledges and keg parties, never experienced all-night-cramming sessions the night before midterms and finals, she knew. As an honor student from the school of hard knocks, a single parent, she had the grades: shades of grey and black, house cleaners majoring in adipose tissue versus muscle, and grades of sanity versus the entire loss thereof. Throughout her years toiling over sweat and regret, Katherine came to understand the intellectual definition as well as the societal prestige accompanying knowledge. From overhearing white adolescents arguing with their parents over competitive grade point averages, she came to know what most Ivy League college admission officers looked for in their school applications. Working as a house-keeper, she developed an informal understanding of the gallery of professional degrees decorating glossy wooden panels she dusted and repositioned. From them, she learned how to recognize creditable Latin words from prestigious universities and colleges where many of the nation's respected doctors, lawyers, and business professionals graduated. From them, she came to know from which prestigious university her beloved son, Mathew, would graduate.

"Did you...?" Her strategic query fell silent to the piercing ring of the telephone.

"I'll get it!"

Katherine threw a leather look his way, halting Mathew in his tracks. Slowly she took a few steps and picked up the phone.

"Hello," Katherine said, in her Standard-American English voice. "Very well, thank you," she said, looking around at Mathew. "Yes, he is. Who may I ask is calling?"

With his head lowered nearly to the ground, Mathew returned to his seat, mumbling. He could feel his windpipe closing, becoming heavier. As if an hourglass swung above his head like a pendulum at its highest arc, lancinating precious seconds, minutes, hours, days, and weeks over his exposed carcass, his breathing slowed to a snail's crawl.

"Oh, how are you?" Katherine continued.

There was a deafening silence, the eternal funeral of not knowing.

"He's eating right now," she said, her eyes grappling with Mathew's hidden anxiety.

Mathew did not move, could not move. Part of him wanted to transmute with the detailed cracks emblazoned on their wooden dining table. The other part thought about simply hiding within the cracks. Not quite deep enough, though.

"Is there a message I can give him? Okay, I will. And thank you, very much," she said, slowly turning away from Mathew. "Goodbye."

With her back facing him, Katherine slowly returned the telephone to its resting place. The moist tuft of dark skin sat regal on the nape of her neck.

Mathew picked up his fork, began to rotate it. Apologetically, the clock sliced through the silence, watching as Mathew nervously attempted to cut into his sausage.

"I know I raised you better! Did you say your grace? I don't care how successful you become in life; don't you *ever* forget to give thanks to the Lord for his blessings!"

A high pitch rang out as the knife and fork fell from Mathew's hands, chiming the edge of his plate. The ring sounded like an orchestra rehearsing for a recital.

"You know it was no one else but the Lord who opened the door for you to be admitted into the University of Pennsylvania. Lord knows; I couldn't do it."

Oh God, Mathew told himself.

"Don't let that Ivy League education come before God! Remember, *you* were born and raised in a *holy* and *sanctified* home. God has been good to you and your mother, and He continues to watch over his flock every step of the way!"

As if he was sitting next to the hallelujah pulpit with those 'preaching ladies' hammering the song 'Go Tell It on the Mountain' down upon his unsaved soul, Mathew sighed.

"What did David mean when he said he would go with you to the tournament, tomorrow?"

Mathew stared quietly into his plate.

"What tournament?" she pushed.

"Mother..."

"Look, you are not going to attend some God-forsaken chess tournament! Do you

hear me? If I've told you once..."

"Will you let me finish?"

"Don't raise your voice to me," pushing her dark, cracked, stubby index finger into his boiling face. "I *am* your mother."

"Will you please... let me finish?"

"Did you really think you could hide this...this scheme of yours about a chess tournament from me? A decent and respectable mother knows *everything* about her children. God gave us that right, the power, the authority."

"Can I finish?"

"Didn't you know that *Mr. University of Pennsylvania*?" Her finger poised to prosecute.

"I know who you are!"

"Then answer your mother!"

"Will *my mother* let her son speak his mind and be his own person?"

"Why? So you can become a lost soul like..."

"Like whom?" Mathew pushed back.

"Answer my question..."

"Say it, *mother.*"

"Don't disrespect your mother," she threw back into his face.

"What's wrong with competing in a chess tournament?"

"Chess is the devil's instrument. It is ungodly! It's no different than gambling! It's an abomination to God!"

"This is not true. Where in the Old or the New Testament is it mentioned that playing chess is an abomination to God?" His jawbone flexed, pupils dilated, chest barreled.

"I will not stand before the Lord on Judgment Day and have to answer for your ungodly behavior."

"I'm not asking you to... Where in the Ten Commandments, or the Beatitudes, is it written 'Woe unto him that participates in a chess match?'"

"Don't mock the Lord!"

"Where...?"

"Did you hear me, Mathew?"

"Where, Mother?"

"What is wrong with you children of today?"

"I'd like to know what's right with our parents," Mathew answered.

"Don't sass your mother... You children think the world revolves around you."

"Then why do you continue to have us?"

"Like death, eggs follow a one-way course."

"Will you answer my question without a sermon, please?" he squeezed through his closed teeth.

"Honor thy mother and thy father…"

"What father?"

Her eyes took further aim, "…that thy days may be *long*…"

"Oh, God," Mathew threw his hands toward the heavens, "here we go."

"…upon the land…"

"What are you afraid of?"

"…which the Lord thy God…"

"This is not about chess or God."

"…giveth thee."

"Are you afraid I'll learn the *white* truth about what happened between you … and my father?"

Before she could grasp another Scripture from the King James text, before she felt her hot, wise blood surging nearly one-hundred-ninety beats per minute through atherosclerotic arteries, Katherine's right hand lashed out and struck Mathew's face with adjudicated authority. The slice of her slap cut into the blandness of their existence like salt to cooked rice. Suddenly, the breath in her exercised lungs tightened up, jarring everything within. Katherine needed a moment. When she could breathe again, she saw the gentle aspect of her maternal heart intercede: the same hand went forth, this time slowly, soft and without scales, reaching to soothe the wound. She hoped to find something to share with him, to say she was sorry, but these words would never come from her lips. It was never possible for her to say such a thing to him, to anyone.

With her loving three-and-a-half-lined signature imprinted in his cheek, slowly Mathew returned his face back to the scathing courtroom. Their eyes collided. Echoes of their disemboweling conversation continued to reverberate loudly throughout her front-row kitchen. A beautiful yellow and brown striped wasp flew into her grease-stained windowpane, floating groggily to the ground. Neither of them heard it, nor noticed it. She stole into his nearly opaque eyes, channeling his heart for shielded secrets. *What is it that you want so desperately? Do you really know what happened some twenty years earlier? Yes, you are entitled to know what really happened. Why is it so difficult? Why, Lord, why?*

As if swept from the outskirts of a hurricane's fury back into the vacuum of a hurricane's eye, Katherine's heart awoke to the spiritual touch of a ghostly hand she barely saw resting sympathetically on her shoulder. However, the fury of the moment wouldn't allow her to fully go there, because deep down inside she knew that door was long since sealed.

Even though their encounter was breath-taking, riveting in fact, profoundly unexpected, even though her head spun as if it were ready to leave the tracks and roll across the floor, collecting crumbs and cockroach parts along the way, nothing could've been more earth-shattering than the presence of that hand upon her shoulders. Katherine jumped so hard that she never noticed her dress tore straight up the back. *Who touched me?* She thought. There was no one there. Like the hand that may have been there, now gone, and like the last breath of her Lord and Savior Jesus Christ nailed to cold pine atop Mount Calvary, so too was Mathew now gone.

Within their small kitchen, empathic objects watched Katherine mourn Mathew's lost meal, his deserted chair. For she might as well have been a lone piece of paper caught within an airshaft which the wind blew playfully hard, tumbling and turning and twisting and rolling along the course of an invisible force that guided her, like a child.

Testimony

Do you have any idea how it feels to be so tired – I mean drained-drawn-and-quartered tired – that the bones of your spirit undergo an out-of-body experience? The kind of dream-state or hallucination or phantasmagoria where you land on the front bench of an ol' Southern Holiness Church, where all the spitting, stomping, shouting, prancing, and convulsing slams you to the mat of your concern like a WWF SmackDown, and sitting next to your captive carcass of creaking bones is that one church lady sitting oh-too-close with her anointed handkerchief, her elastic water-proof bible, and that scruffy Nightclub voice, wailing against soulful rhythms from an imaginary, sultry saxophone sermon.

You know the type, those testa-lying saints, discreetly seasoned by undocumented graces, *The View* spaces, and non-DNA traces from undisclosed places. Intimately smudged with pan-lipped memories from a very different life; Christian-ladies who graduated magna cum laude from Aunt Esther's Holiness College.

Yes, the type that arrives every Sunday morning early, sits on the front row in the same spot, and, after every thought-provoking point delivered from the Preacher, as if tag-teamed by the almighty Holy Spirit, takes to the floor with a halleluiah gymnastic cartwheel; her dress trying to keep up, she back-flips in bloomer fashion, hysterically signifying, convulsively waving, suffocating you with her praise-da-Lord perfume, shouting in her do-me-now spirit – ending with "I heard dat!!!" Perfect-ten stance.

As if that wasn't enough for my delusional state of being, and without ever taking a break to exit to the nearest ladies' room, she falls back into her seat to catch her much-needed, un-minted breath, with discreet I-hope-this-garter-is-holding-up commotion, and continues with rocking and reeling and spiritual rapping. All the while, unmerciful thoughts begin to take shape, as I entertain thoughts about using my torn panty hose as a hanging noose for this lady's halleluiah-neck.

And while I continue to duck under her slashing handkerchief, her Muhammad Ali bible, and anything else flying up from under her Smithsonian Institute dress, two pulpit preachers jump up and heave their 'guilty-as-sin finger' just a few inches away from my nose, yelling 'I know what you did last summer.'

Oh, really? Or were you still undergoing withdrawals from those unmentionable laces your smegma prayerfully tasted last night? Anointing Sister-who-cares' chapters with a hard-lined scripture from the pulpit to the bench, from the wine to the door, from the hotel receipt to the floor, from Sodom to I-want-some-more. And while it remains terribly impossible to concentrate on any one preacher, especially the scriptural meaning embodying their sermon, with my bones and processing racked where this 'do-me-now' lady has obviously contributed to my decision to just say the hell with it all, suddenly two offering trays with the words "WE WANT IT ALL, NOW!" etched along its bottom, are shoved into my face.

With one hand rubbing my terribly throbbing temple, I couldn't resist the moment to question: "Would it have been any worse if I took Satan up on his offer for a ride in his new fully loaded Mercedes Benz S-Class?"

Well Water

At the still point of the turning world. Neither flesh nor fleshless.
Neither from nor towards; at the still, there is the dance . . .

— T. S. Eliot, "Burnt Norton" (1943)

Upon the road of rock
fruit: flower: pink brassieres:
splash like tongues networking Golden Calves:
  Substantia Nigra

        Every drop of sex —
        Within a prefix of water —
        Motherboards crest —

Every Sunday morning   i go to church wearing torn blue genes
always   frothing with Eve's cache
always   outside the delicious unstrung harp
always   where Song of Songs dance 21° of separation:
  Ceteris Paribus

        Christ —
        Christie's —
        Cormorants —

i tasted its sweet cracking crunches
i ate the ripened heart of Pardes
i understand why quilted diaries & underwear-bread whisper

How surprising is this   when God
constipated from Creation   never accepts His prescription
always   failing to flush the toilet
always   failing to wash His hands
always   the Genesis of Revelations:
  Hapax Legomena

        Satan —
        Sotheby's —
        Swans —

While   trilling violins
            breast feed
                disobedient waterfalls

RACISM

The Blood of Rain

Drowning in meadow-spoken roots, I reach for heartfelt songs, once, so rich with oxygenated virtues, twice, so free from an unforgiving life. Songs gleaned from salvific tomatoes, flowing sweet the Nile. Voyages imprismed as a glint refracted without blink, without smile, messages to splat against something, anything – life-supporting droplets passed with grass concern, lawn pity. What was there: a bed of crabs to obscure the analgesic dirt, the antiperspirant stench, the grandeur embodying a crimson stance. Like knuckles half-curled, tapping on the drum of a shack, shadow of a room existing as a postal address with but one letter in the box, this song of rain continues to pour dry. Behind closed mores, I lick deliberate snowfalls, wrangled after birth. What did this mean? From where does this floodwater spring? My cup remains half-filled, cracks lining its bottom have laid their webs. I watch reminiscent musings of pellets fall, nerve endings teleconference heme & beryl-blues & female & globin & woman & man & child, all raced by fashionable weather, as I drown, listening to the pulsations of torrential veils.

Why am I so thirsty?

Nystagmus

"In God's name, please let me go!"

The roar of laughter echoed throughout the cabin space of the big, tarnished former school bus as it sped along forgotten roads, maneuvered through grazing shadows.

"What have I done to you?" Exhausted tears streamed down across her naked, low-hanging breasts, pausing for a peek over the buxom divide, and then diving from dilated nipples out into a dark, twisting, inguinal taking.

"Please, I beg you..."

With a wave of high-fives, jovial clapping, and pumped fists, the laughter continued.

"Whose move?"

"Mine."

"No, it's my turn."

A sharp embankment reeled them laterally, momentarily silencing their play.

"Help me!" With gray and black hair frayed, matted about taut roots. Her lashed expression, coarse, a fervent affirmation canvassed before a windswept concerto willowing from within, suddenly she was reminded why the caged bird sings. "Somebody please...help."

"Shhh...," he said, eyeballing the careless clock and the neon sign – **First Place Prize** – glaring above her. "If you don't mind, we're trying to finish our chess tournament."

"Check!" Slamming his offensive piece into position.

She took solemn inventory of their blue-eyed faces, same scaly smiles, same deceptive tone, and same Venus flytrap expression hovering over their chess games. No one seemed to care that she was a middle-aged woman restrained in the nude, with a plastic bag sitting at her feet. No one seemed to care she was the only person of color on this seemingly routeless bus. What everyone did seem to care about was who would win her tender soul.

"Please, someone help me...," she mumbled. Trying once again to free her stretch-marked play-dough flesh. Suddenly, the long yank of the metal brake, dragged their attention alongside the bus's jolting halt.

"Ah, come on..."

"What gives?"

"Why are we stopping?"

"What now?" they all shouted at the driver.

Up and out from under the huge steering wheel, the legs of the driver came. An elderly man with glasses, peppered hair on each side of his head, and air-filled khaki pants with brown docksides. Hanging out just above the long flapping black leather belt around his small waist, he wore a gray button-down that somehow managed to stay with his small physique. Outside of his eyes, which were firmly set under the heavy underbrush of slanted brows, he had an ordinary face. After obtaining his walking staff behind his seat, he turned towards his passengers and their captive, steadied himself for the long walk towards the back of the bus.

"He's coming this way!"

A parade of hands flew up, covering their blue eyes like a salute to an officer passing in review. "Don't look into his eyes," one of them whispered.

His presence, his ascetic demeanor, proverbial and serene, like the hypnotic comfort from a thick blanket during the ear-rattling bite of winter, violated their natural guise. He knew the color of their glory, those vespers enveloping their deeds, and he had what it took to make them mind. With the brunt of his staff carefully tapping the rubber mat, his steps slow, deliberate. Like a monk traversing hallowed halls of the Sistine Chapel, he passed every eight by eight chessboard. The reflection of his passage from the inside windows stared back at him with a sovereign nod. An indelible sigh escaped as he came upon her. With her head down, defeated, she saw feet. *Were they His sandals*

*that were riddled with the scorched sands of man's misery and scorn,
and dread and sin? Have I no water to wash His feet? Have I no water...*

She looked up. The glint in her excavated eyes was cavernous,
brittle as glass. Her thick lips nearly glued from the accumulated
phlegm, endless frustration. She struggled to speak, to see, just be
free.

"Can you help me?"

He placed one hand on her shoulder, "Rise, and sin no more."

To the disgust of the blue-eyed Chess competitors, whose
mumbles and groans stirred the airspace, she delivered her cracked,
smudged glass upon his shores. While droplets of tears and various
compositions of water scrambled from her shadowed crack, she
graciously watched as he cradled the brim of her empty glass, wiped
it clean of grime and smudges, and then returned it to her with
stigmata eyes.

"This is not my stop?"

"This stop will not be yours to visit again, but you are here."

"Where shall I go?"

With deep-set eyes, which looked as if all of time had once been
cradled, he answered with a silent gift she placed within her bag, to
open sometime later.

"But I'm all alone. May I sit with you?"

After looking around at *them*, eyes cowering from his reproach,
he said, "How long will you cast your rubies before swine?"

With dark cheeks and subcutaneous flab jiggling, her bag shot into
her arms as she turned and galloped sideways down the thin aisle. In
haste to alight from her brush with *them*, passing ever so close to their
salivating jowls, she boldly flung her bag and warfare hips into the
columns of chess boards laden with brilliant tactics, casting all of *their*
competitive efforts before the rights of just cause, as flaming exple-
tives followed sharply in her wake.

Once off the bus, she couldn't help but smile. She looked back for
him. He was there, sitting in the driver's seat, waving like a departing
old friend. As for the others – *them* – she watched their high-browed
faces pressed against the greasy glass of that mobile prison. She
watched in unimaginable horror as *their* azure pupils remained fixed
on her, *their* mouths moving, spewing vile maledictions and eternal

execrations capable of burning the sun. Then, like the memory of a memory, the bus was gone, and so was her smile.

Centered nowhere, a molecule of disparity lost in a sea of illusory white clouds, an unnerving guest-of-honor seated before the precipice of a timeless plan, with no idea where she was, no one to talk to, and nothing at all in sight, she stood. What is this place?

Like an abandoned lighthouse, she stood amid her existence, a displaced pebble washed onto a sandless beach of abject nothingness, waiting for the rest of time to realize what a mistake it had made. Hoping. But before she could think another thought, ask another question, take in another breath, a lurid mist, pearl in color, slithered about her person, undulated through the rib of her design, sniffed at her still moist pubic hair, unearthed her footsteps from before, chimed her stapled unfamiliarity, then moved in to announce to the rest, she had finally arrived.

Where am I? She whispered.

You are here, with us.

Where are you?

We've always been with you.

Why am I here?

No answer.

As she remained locked in the web of an unfounded inspection, a sturdy breeze whirled in with a reprimanding force and the mist released her. Far off, a loud crack sounded. She was lost to it all, as the weight of an authoritative gavel struck hard against the investigative ennui and the postmodern glimmer fueled by loud cell phone conversations, urban aromas, unrealistic introspections, inappropriate anticipations, and a myriad of precipitous meetings and deadlines. All of this invaded her reasoning. Everybody and everything comprising the international milieu of a bustling downtown New York City took light.

The World Trade Center memorial –

New York Stock Exchange Green –

NYPD blue –

Two-wheeled yellow streaks –

Black rallies –

White concerts –

Phalanx of brownstones –
Homeless grey –
Orange conventions –
Purple parades –
Central Park silver –
Red sirens –
Yellow politicians –
Hey Joe!
Where's my train?
This is my bus?
How will I pay my bills?
Taxi!
You BASTARD!
Up yours!
Whatever!

In the aromatic fumes burning from millenniums past, she felt dazed by the beat in their steps, the rhythmic sway in their dance. Everything intoxicated her, filled her with the verve of a new boyfriend. For a moment, without a care in her world, she stood smiling, imbibing the delirium of a shadowed Roman Empire. Hail, she followed, thinking she knew the true intent of a baseless society – carpe diem. The "Blue Pill' was handed over and swallowed freely. All of this she tasted wondrously, until she looked down and discovered that the rusty figure of a dry snail clamoring under her weathered shell was gone.

She looked upon herself in utter shock, stunned. She had no rational answer to support what she saw. Did I accidentally rub Aladdin's lamp? She was twenty-five years younger, curvaceous, and ripe for the picking. She reached up and touched her hair. It rolled around softly onto her shoulders, strands vibrant with the shimmering silk of youth, once again black and accommodatingly long, real, and strong. Further down, she felt the peripheral tingling against the rock-cold pavement. And like a spider lounging upon its webbed prey, fat, hairy, and happy, she saw her vital elixir of youth, the foundation of her human *self* indignantly sucked from the soles of her feet, everything once again given away.

She didn't want old age, death. Anything but this, she thought. No longer did she find this veiled hedonism and its deceptive aroma alluring, no longer attractive, and no longer did the music of their dance speak to her prudent wants and reasonable desires. There was nothing about *them* she wanted. There was nothing she could glean from their devouring folly. She had had enough. Unfortunately, the same could not be said for *them*.

As she struggled to divorce herself from their deceiving guise, their unhealthy nature, a contemptuous beam of unknown brilliance focused down upon her. There she remained, ruminating, unceremoniously naked, speaking in tongues.

Durn My Hide

It's all a farce, – these tales they tell about the breezes sighing,
and moans astir o'er field and dell because the year is dying.
— Paul Laurence Dunbar, *Merry Autumn*, (1913)

Sun beatin down with magnilyin eye, watchin me hard, like Mister. Flies be wippin in & out, smellin me with da lash, i be durn ef dem federate mozskitoz aint skeered of my black hide. Always flyin bout my beads, always lookin down at me. i be durn ef doz hot chains aint pressin gainst my skin. Nuttin worse den tryin ta breave in skillets uv fire. Hits hell i say. Nuttin butt hell!

'Taint much ta see sittin here on a graveyaud poach, breavin nigga air, loose boa'd air, list'nin ta rusted ol boa'ds crack & moan like whiskey mule bones loozin' splinters. Da cott'n & wheat & grass, dey all look bout da same. Got mo color den i eber had. Yon i hyear da trees fixin ta laff. Been whisperin & laffin at me ere year. Not yet a loose boa'd, aint cut, still livin free. Butt choo wait, cum time wen da firplace be hungrey. Luk at cha, not sayin much wit dem leaves pokin hits mouf.

i be durn ef i aint got butt one shew. Whear hit gone? 'Taint much ta say wit one tung. i be durn if hit aint got tired of flappin, tired uv waitin fo me ta move & jus hop-on like Kunta. Whatcha gon do? Shew strings & woe-men. Trippin up & steppin on, aint nuttin butt da same. Yup, i reckon hits bout dat time uf da year. i can hyear tween my legs, in ma feet. Stikay words, cott'n paste toes talkin bout hot & slow dayz. Yup, i hyear ya comin up da Nile road, draggin yo big ol brogan brehsts, pullin & puffin & diggin & scatchin & lookin & wavin. is dat my shew? Durn my hide ef dat aint chew i smell. Like a rooster callin ere body ere moanin, hit ken tell time.

Durn my hide ef ya aint fixin ta make us niggas grits & white sand, & what fo? 'Taint no use tryin ta poe white sand over black eye peas. Durn my hide ef hit aint hell walkin round all dem loose boa'ds.

Dust Wed, Splinter Spit

Dust in my eye, cotton pupils picked. Watching myself; waiting to see what everybody else did not want to see – me walking, be talking, dropping the shade on an open casket, sweeping the view. Damn it, lost another one! Won't get too many more chances, cuz' lady luck can be a bitch when she wants to be.

I am married to a skinny broom, carrying a flat-ass pan. No dress, no legs, and no hips. Good morning honey. Good night dear. Broomstick and pan are all I know. My days are filled with me holding and squeezing a broom and pan. Breathing dust, living with splinter spit. Everybody knows her, but she belongs to me. Everybody knows where she lives, but I am the one who always must get her. Everybody got somebody but grinning and teeth is all I see coming from them when we are together. My broom and pan know these pockets of hands, this visible smell, these mule bones. Like spit to ground, we have been together a long time. No arguing, no fussing, just dust wed, splinter spit.

In the beginning, it was Moses hard. No commandments, just Pharaohs and sandstone dust. Time and living with nothing have a way of making things soft. You get used to having nothing. It won't kill ya'. Like a good old shoe, dirty Fruit of the Looms, time makes everything feel much better.

I have a dream

Panther Lurking High Above the Hood

Black

in the day

swollen toes look up

wonderin' what

other gonna do

With flat affect

two sole brothers

watchin' each other

wonderin' why

this world so cold

Black

in the day

feats don't

fail me

now

Silent as Impression Made by Stone

Silent   as an impression   made by stone

Black onyx flamed with writings   to go gentle   in the night

So it is that I   a Mysterious Traveler   walk this way alone

In this silence   I sit on the side   of the dirt bone

Waiting at the edge   of the black line   of the farthest woods

Silent   as an impression   made by stone

Where all who believe   this   sarcophagus sown

Well into the hands   of Osiris and Ra   as mummies

So it is that I   a Mysterious Traveler   walk this way alone

All but a water lily   speaks   in the shadow   of a lotus tone

I go formless   shadowing-less   across wading waters   tarrying

Silent   as an impression   made by stone

Delivered   on parchment paper   to a mass of one

This message   driven from   essence long since gone

So it is that I   a Mysterious Traveler   walk this way alone

In my will   take this much   without loan

Paint me   crate me   canvas this I say

So it is that I   a Mysterious Traveler   walk this way alone

Exodus

What if Jesus had said, "All right, you can be white-trash
or a nigger or ugly"!
— Flannery O'Connor, "Revelation" (1964)

Summertime. Alabama is always as precious as a Sunday morning pulpit, preaching cotton sweat, generational sin.

Around me, the Stepin-Fetchit air shuffled along, with a shoulder-shrugging giggle. Every so often, an aroma of rootlessness marched up my nostrils, down the back of my throat. Its smell raw, ruled space.

"God don't like niggers!" the policeman yelled as he placed handcuffs around my tiny wrists. He had a dull, white, pug-nosed face. His eyes seemed too close together, grainy. The inside of his mouth, like feet of family that walked away. He moved with deliberate enjoyment.

"How come dez people don't wear shoes, Bubba?" his partner growled from the other side of the police car.

"I 'on't know, Jeb," Bubba replied, beneath a hat that fit around the meat of his head like the snap of a Southern Black women's purse.

I hate police, their false uniforms, the smugness tattooed to their faces. What makes them any different from those hooded fools burning crosses, looking to catch one of us for their Saturday night lynching party.

"How ol' you, boy?" he continued.

I looked up at eyes that flickered at the farthest point of a cave. I could almost hear the whisper of a grumbling wind groping a shafted space, pacing as it bounced off crusted edges of a Cro-Magnon era. I could almost follow his diet for the last few days, of grease and fat and cider and beer. There was a little of each chiseled into the fabric of his tortured uniform. Inching out from his right pants pocket, just under the husk of belly flab sprawling over his belt buckle, the head of a small key attached to its keyring, peaked out. I wondered...

"You mighty young for such a thang as...," Bubba said as if standing at a window, gazing down on his plantation.

"Who you wit?" Jeb interrupted.

With the enrolment of morning complete, I listened to soprano crickets slice through jagged rays of sunlight. I listened to a sonata of guttural and mating calls, a fusion of tweets and fluttering, nature whispering under the hum and drone of a sticky-underwear day. All of this was listened to as a lecture; speaking to what I was, to what I would soon become, to what I needed to do.

"Who put chu' up to this, nigger?" Bubba pressed.

I wanted to say something. Amidst the festering and scheming and whirling within me, I said nothing.

"Do ya' hear me, boy?" jamming his pigmy forefinger into his meat temple.

I continued to watch the Alabama dirt road lick the sky.

On my right, a battalion of corn stalk reeled gently in formation. On the other side, jagged lines of barbed-wire fence scaled for miles around arable farmland. While polygons of wood lounged against the barroom rays of sun and shine, off in the distance patches of cows and horses grazed along a staggering landscape.

I inhaled the funeral parlor air; its diminishing tones needling through the Sabbath of day. I thought about the nature of nothingness, its gaping sustenance so ripe with time, how often it registered the passing of wind wuthering, of cascading chaos. Lost in the adolescence of wonderment, I thought about the passing of a ship, its sails lapping in the tasteless wind. Where pale blue thoughts cradled my mast, commanded my nautical will to steer further away, steer into the day of another...

But because I was always a failure, sinking was the only thing I knew. I knew the meaning of drowning, the inability to walk above debilitating dreams, cancerous desires straddling my every being like the crew from a pirate ship glaring down my throat, breathing their colonial beer-breath into my face, rocking their rum-soaked eyes back and forth like a pendulum from the highest arc. Maddening it all was, to stand on the bow of a ship only I manned. Deafening it all was, to continuously walk ad hoc planks, wobbling splinters, only to be returned each time aboard this ship of heavenly demise.

I looked at his swollen belly working against tightly-pulled buttons in a stained, State-issued police uniform. His hidden waistline, his sagging pants, dingy and wrinkled, dusty flat shoes with overturned soles that probably couldn't wait to run away if given the chance. All of him I watched, as his long slender shadow seemed to make fun of him behind his back.

"… ya' hear me, boy?"

Under the poetry of a captive hell, I stared into his Jack-o-Lantern face, those Halloween eyes. I spoke to him with the loudest silence I could ever have yelled, as I managed to bend my arms, lower my head to scratch my neck.

"Nigger, what's wrong with yo' neck?"

"I's fifteen," I finally let go.

"Whatchu' say?" Bubba said, as the back of his rusty hand went hard across my face.

Struggling to lift myself up from what seemed like the longest fall, I felt something warm, sweet, slip from the edge of my lips. My head rang. My eyes felt as if they wanted to roll away.

"Speak up, boy!" Bubba screamed.

"I's fifteen, sir."

"Well, looka here, Jeb," Bubba said, as he leaned over to release a piece of his dark, gooey soul, "this monkey can talk."

After the air in my lungs returned, the road was once again all there, I watched a tar-like substance squirt from what seemed like the edge of his soul, slap the proud blank face of ancient dirt. Mesmerized by its Nileness, I looked deep into the heart of the black spit sitting in the dirt, as it refused to congeal with a newly formed member of another.

"That's a good one, Bubba," Jeb yelled, laughing something ugly. "Hit him 'gain."

Like tongue to a rusty nail, their fun sent shivers up my spine. There was something about their laughter that sucked the marrow from my bones, pushed something up just below my balls into the lower portions of my intestines, on into the superior aspect of my chest, and then to the back of my throat where it settled, with a heavy metallic taste.

All I needed to do, just a bit closer, closer, to touch the key to freedom...

Once again I bent my arms, lowered my head to scratch my neck.

"Nigga, what's wrong with yo' neck?" Jeb yelled, as he came closer. "Lemme' see what's..." taking the liberty to grab the back of my neck.

The trap had been set, tripped, and now it was time to ensnare the prey... As I suspected, his movements were flat-footed, feverously slow. Feeling his approach without looking, waiting with the intent of the deadliest spider, I held my breath.

<hr>

It was getting hotter. Beads of sweat slipped down my black face, itched as they glided along the center of my back.

Bubba was like a wilting clump of clay. I could not resist the urge to slap his face, watch his head wobble like hog fat. The handcuffs continue to sway from my left wrist as I paused to steal a moment from priceless records. Not for the sake of pausing did I do so, nope, I paused because I needed to swish the bitter sand slipping through my sunken hourglass. I needed to hold the brazen steam escaping from my hot air balloon. I paused to swallow the moment, freely.

Not far away, the knife I gave Jeb stood straight up from his silent chest. Like one of the crucified lost, his arms lay outstretched. He looked so peaceful.

With nothing to halt my purpose, nothing to disarm my natural intent, I walked over to Bubba, sprawled on his back. I took his meaty hand, curled our forefingers around the trigger of the .38 revolver, plopped my tongue to one side of my mouth, and then I slowly placed the gun's barrel alongside his temple. The reason for this: I wanted to sit and watch him, watch his ship take to the gales of a one-way course. A few feet away, his wad of tobacco sat wrapped in dirt. I looked into his mouth, now alive with color. I needed to scratch, run my fingers along the side of my neck. As I did so, dark-grey cakes of sweat and grime gathered under what was left of my fingernails.

In both our hands, like the feel of a King cobra raised with its forked tongue constantly tasting the air of intent, its fangs poised with the venom of purpose, its blackness alive with unimaginable might, the cold .38 lay, waiting. I felt its power surging up my arm into the foreground of my left brain, where it sank its fangs, riveting with sheer madness, deafening delight.

"There will never be a place in heaven for niggers...," Bubba uttered.

Like a whirlwind, everything proceeded like the beginning of time. "There was light!" I wasn't sure if I was here, if I was breathing, if this really was a dream and I just couldn't wake up. But the weight of the gun and the warmth from his hands and the smell of the pulsating blood said otherwise.

Within an instance, together we pulled back on the soft trigger. There was a feeling of ease, then the explosion of a signed contract, a fatal covenant. The sound was like no other, the release was like no other, as it tore a path straight through the both of us. With eyelids nearly pulled over my head, I fell over on my back.

On my knees, I was hypnotized by the spill of shattered brain emblazoned upon the long, thirsty road, completely enthralled by its orchestrated rubies, so rich with oxygenated songs. My temples swiveled against the sight of a pomegranate emblazoned upon the long, rasping shore. I couldn't help but think about the spill, the color of rubies, so rich with oxygenated songs. Songs flowing sweet like sugarcane, pulsing without blink, without smile, messages in the motion of its inevitable splat against something plain, needing it, calling it.

Against my shirt, blood droplets landed with grass concern, lawn pity. I touched it, rolled the hushed, red snowfall over my fingers. It was beautiful. I lifted it towards my nose. The smell of warm snow danced inside my mind as I saw my grey matter churn, move like ships against seafaring storms.

Yes, there I was, on board, the only member of a descending voyage, grappling with my shelf of self, holding tightly to whatever was near, the mast of now, the bow of then, something, anything – pushing away ravaging waves. From everywhere, histories unborn with salt came. I was drenched with knowledge of a threatening kind. Its might struck hard. I was thrown, heard its rage, fell from stage. Where is land? Must find ground, touch the shore. My breath was taken, given back, and then taken again.

As loud as my lungs could, a primordial scream was released into the backward mouth of my heritage. A few seconds later, eyes opened to a meadow of stalks spreading before tongue-shaped leaves. Halfway up and unfurling at the tip, red, blue, or yellow petals marked with spots of color that rose upon the surface, and from the red, blue, or yellow gloom of the throat emerged a straight bar, rough with gold dust and slightly clubbed at the end. The petals were voluminous enough to dance with the summer breeze, and when they moved, the red, blue, and yellow lights passed one over the other, staining an inch of the brown earth beneath with a spot of the most intricate color.

After what seemed like hours, but simply a minute, I exhaled, because I knew Bubba and Jeb were now alive with the eternal blessing of knowledge and understanding. Because the marrow from my bones had returned to its rightful place, I exhaled and stood as the warm rising sun congratulated my back, saying, *Job well done.*

In the end, I tried to breathe deeply, I tried not to reach up and scratch my neck, but it was too late. Like so many times before, I sat alone, a shadow listening to dark voices, fully participated in the turning in on myself. Privy to the dense awfulness of an artificial nigger inhaling dingy sheets too many times fallen from bayou clotheslines. Even I could not stand my smell. However, I was covered with the best of the worst, intoxicated beyond anything my little inexperienced life could ever have imagined. Like Adam and Eve after tasting forbidden fruit, I felt whole; sinfully baptized in the power of the flesh.

I ran towards Bubba, grabbed his revolver, shoved it into my pocket, threw the other one on the front seat of the police car, and without wiping my hands, my face, I jumped in, listened to the ignition roar, released the brake, floored the accelerator pedal, and left the crime scene, with a golden plume of dust spreading upward as I watched in the rear-view mirror.

Down through what seemed like the tail end of a flat umbilical cord, with nothing but the nosy wind licking my brain, I drove.

Driving shoeless, the memory of colors – red, blue, green, bright orange, and yellow – the gripping aroma of a bleeding self was dizzying. A few times, I nearly pulled over, maybe just for a moment to gather my wits, but something compelled me to press on, keep moving.

Every now and then, I popped my head out of the car window. Every time, there was the same thing: nothing. What was the meaning behind all of this? Who would imagine I could spill blood on a Sunday morning? Half of the blue, landscaped sky answered with a languid expression. The other half seemed to shrug its puffed shoulders, utterly nonplussed. I became the child of these thoughts as the road dipped and swung through back-door towns and hyperactive stretches of stuttering highway.

Ahead, acres of fences, the tundra of farmland flanked the drowning Southern landscape. Everywhere the long, wide skirts of forests swished and swayed, but seldom were there folks. With the window down, the tiny specks of blood dried, pulling and tugging on thick, dark skin. Inside my head, the concert was over. I glanced down and saw how the blood specks seemed to meld with my shirt and pants. This was too strange. I thought about what lay ahead, what my life had become. Did I really know? I wonder if I ever really cared. I just wanted to prolong this great feeling, to never let it go away, never to feel the way those two police officers made me *feel*, never again.

I wanted to discover the full range of human experience, answers to questions surrounding the glory of unchained flesh. Along the right shoulder of endless roads, there was a sea of white mailboxes. The gravel racing beneath the car whispered along like momma's lullaby, remembered in the hush of the winding eve. I was going sixty, sometimes seventy. Going where? The dignity of time prevailed like a tall glass of mint julep laced with cyanide. The unknown was frightening. I was leaving behind all things familiar. All these things were never really a true memory of value. Along the way, this stretch of gravel and dust was nothing more than a passage through life itself, a road for all to walk or stumble across, or simply die trying.

There was a natural luxury to the hum while driving down the road, slicing through the fine sweetness of Southern perfumes – Camellias, begonias, magnolias, hydrangeas – that seem to paint the world. Under this alluring spell of automobile rubber and hard, open road, time was lost, only to be awakened by the unfortunate fact that the car was slowing down, now puttering along.

Out of gas and without any sign of a filling station within sight, I was slapped back into a tessellated reality. How could this be? Did I check their pockets for money, maybe a credit card? No! Damn! I slammed the steering wheel, hard. There was the gun, but nothing else in the police car. I parked the car on the side of the road, closer in towards the underbrush of ever-leaf and overgrowth.

Hell!

I was lost, and I felt stupid for not paying attention to the signs along the way. Yes, everything had passed like a blur, but still, that was no excuse. I got out of the car. Standing in the faint, fresh air felt good. It was different and refreshing, like a long warm, bath. I looked around. Thick, green landscape everywhere. The hot breath of the spectral wickedness of woods stared back into my face. "Don't ever go into the woods!" I remember hearing from those I once called family. "The woods are not meant for our kind. We swing from their trees!"

Purging my mind of this nauseous memory, I stood at its foreboding doorway. It's delicious scent deceiving, purely natural. The wine of a summer morning poured through the vintage breeze. It was palpable with the afterthought of a fresh rain, and it reeked of conifers, mulch, and southern longleaf pine. Through the dense vault of minuscule shapes and shadows, through this village of pulsing willow, carefully, cautiously, my fingers digging against the side of my neck, digging with nails I forgot were bittern off yesterday, and the day before, I pressed.

The sun was a shimmering yellow and the melody of heat reverberated with a stereophonic lash. Everything was dry and crackly, a feeling of constipation, as I pushed through the child-like vines and thick brush tugging at my pants and thighs. I listened to the dense, green hell of tormented, grey trees, of rattling Camellia leaves. Everywhere, alien mating calls, the humming of bees and dragonflies, everything alive, breathing. Every now and again, my footsteps met with solid footing. A gaggle of gnats and flies and bees and mosquitoes hovered close to the sweet scent of black heat, hoping to sample the still-wet currency of life soaked into my shirt, caked into my mule-bone hide. Swatting at them, trying to wave them off, but they managed to stay the course. Soon thereafter, when I thought it could not get any worse, my stomach chimed in, and not too far behind, thirst raised its ugly head.

Desperation was the attire of the moment. I could feel its weight as my pulse and respirations raced. I felt myself succumbing to the will of the forest. I looked around, a few feet that way, nothing. Every direction seemed to open towards the same verdant wasteland. Thoughts of the forest asking *Who are you?* raced through my head. *What are you doing in our forest?*

I did not answer.

Through the photosynthetic slough, sunlight squeezed. Oblique silhouettes reached all around me. The high shrill of cicadas continue to bleed into the warm breeze. My concern over hunger, thirst, even the fact that I was lost, suddenly fell silent as my heart snapped.

Hell!

I felt a cold stubborn rage come over me. Licking my lips, trying to gather what morsel of breath remained, I ran. My mind tried to catch up, my lungs felt as if I was standing on them. Tiny little eyes appeared to rub up against me, embers of pandemonium focusing in. I nearly fell.

To make it through grass nearly as tall as trees, I needed to lift my knees, to jump higher. I gave it my best, stretching and lifting as much as I could, but the forest was not designed for sprinters. It was an obstacle course for hurdlers with strong thighs. Despite a maddening laughter, the need to catch my breath way ahead of me, I managed to capture some distance. But to where? I was still lost.

The handcuffs continued to flip and chime. Had I concentrated more on making it through the dense brush, rather than worrying about dark forest warnings, I probably would have avoided the out-stretched arm of a low-hanging oak tree branch. Completely engaged in my fury, turning around and looking left and then right, I slammed into it, headfirst. Immediately, the gun, large beads of sweat, especially my hyperventilating, erupted like loose bowels.

Beneath this ancient, pulpit-preaching xylem, baptizing phloem, across this Eden of moss, fern, twigs, and freshly disturbed dirt, like paint stuck to a feather, a color not meant for any canvas, but cracked residue hanging off the edge of an unthumbed palette, I lay outstretched. Something as powerful as lightning had touched me, reached deep down into my lost soul, calmed ravaging waters. Then, the numbing discussion of a whispering breeze.

Not far away, I heard my home's screen door slam, the sound of running water in the kitchen. Is dinner ready, momma? The house always smells funny this time of year – mothballs and old plastic coverings. Memories of school bells, schoolchildren rushing to get outside, church-sermon change rolling in offering trays, the choir shouting "Hallelujah," as the preacher speaks in tongues, the sound of leaves growing far from shades of green, orange, and yellow, long flapping sheets dancing before a gravid sky, Clorox blue.

To open towards solid, realizing ground, to reach out towards the helm of my ship, I tried to scratch my neck, but the struggle was too great. Through the thick roof of Camellia leaves, castigating pine, a blazing, pitiless glare of sheltered sky rippled.

A storm was approaching.

It was so beautiful, so different.

residue hanging off the edge of an unthumbed palette, I lay out-stretched. Something as powerful as lightning had touched me, reached deep down into my lost soul, calmed ravaging waters. Then, the numbing discussion of a whispering breeze.

Not far away, I heard my home's screen door slam, the sound of running water in the kitchen. Is dinner ready, momma? The house always smells funny this time of year – mothballs and old plastic coverings. Memories of school bells, schoolchildren rushing to get outside, church-sermon change rolling in offering trays, the choir shouting "Hallelujah," as the preacher speaks in tongues, the sound of leaves growing far from shades of green, orange, and yellow, long flapping sheets dancing before a gravid sky, Clorox blue.

To open towards solid, realizing ground, to reach out towards the helm of my ship, I tried to scratch my neck, but the struggle was too great. Through the thick roof of Camellia leaves, castigating pine, a blazing, pitiless glare of sheltered sky rippled.

A storm was approaching.

It was so beautiful, so different.

RELATIONSHIPS

Rivers Beneath My Pillow

Desiring truth, awaiting it, laboriously distilling a few words, forever desiring—(a cry starts to the left, another to the right. Wheels strike divergently. Omnibuses conglomerate in conflict)—forever desiring.
— Virginia Woolf, Monday or Tuesday (1921)

When I lay my head upon my pillow at night, I hear something. Not the normal things you might expect someone to hear in the hush of the winding eve with aging woes from squeaking bones and creaking rafters, tiny whiffs from a caravan of veils, personal recaps from the dramatic hum and gossip circulating under office whispers that you can't wait to get home to spit into your telephone – "Girl, you won't believe what happened today..." – about the dog or cat or child or husband or Mother or Father, or someone else you know who was involved in some unexpected ordeal or circumstance involving the yard, the couch, to the chair, at the bus stop, in the lunch room, in the class room, or something that was said at the office, or perhaps, if the Sun is rising in Taurus, and the Moon is going from Leo into Virgo, and all unemployed shadows and inconsiderate shades have retired to their undisclosed vault of smoke and alternative mirrors, and all else is well within the rotational axis of the stars and other moons coming into the gravitational voice of our solar system, and after the gleaning of exhausted thoughts and the ingestion of a hearty meal has done more than hit the right spot, and when the operatic octaves and tenors from that cow-dung ranch of confrontational emotions and exercised jaw muscles stand fully in remission, and, all arms and hands flapping and waving like birds navigating flight have settled onto a compromising veil of lowered eyebrows and levelled diastolic/systolic readings, then maybe, just maybe, I might have a chance to dine in the breathe-taking, eye-rolling penetration of a hard-veined log between hairy-lipped, speaking hips, babbling in crackling pulses from the intoxicating aroma of wood aflame with tip-cream to kindle my ruby hearth, making me whole, not a Black Hole, but a worm hole.

And, after the heart climaxes from its percussive swing dance and octopussy fingers and Eastern Diamondback tongue and nose and saliva and the grunts and groans and the name-calling and pushing-n-pulling have all *Gone With The Wind*, and the only things remaining are the lingering ventilations patrolling graveyards, then hopefully I might swallow a therapeutic, needful sleep, where many other dreams...

But no, this is not what I hear swimming through my external auditory canal, lapping at the shores of my tympanic membrane, breast stroking my nerves with a cacophony of whines, begging to enter for a sharp rest in the temporal thorns of my punitive bed. This is not the type of thing my sensitive ears draw in, telling me, "Sleep, baby girl, everything is going to be all right," because I know it's not; it hasn't been all right for a long, long, long time.

Do you know why?

For, I have yet to know what it's like to experience a day when my mind speaks to me in a normal, healthy way. A day complete with genuine smiles or bus-stop questions or grocery-store conversations about the nature and philosophy of current events, maybe postulating on the psychosocial impact of immoral technology and its debilitating effects on our down-trodden society.

I'd like to know what it's like to walk down the street during the spring or summer seasons, and not have little flying insects – bees, flies, wasps, gnats, mosquitoes, anything small and with wings – fly directly into me, as if I wasn't there. Better still, I'd like to know why birds never pass by me without turning their inquisitive heads and eyes to look directly at me, as if they know me. Can you tell if this is a temporary condition of life, or am I living a human existence Nature has yet to assimilate?

I'd like to know how it feels to answer a telephone and not hear my voice ask from the other end, "What do you want?" I'd like to know how to make friends without folk-smoke hissing at my ankles, mouth, vagina, and wallet. I'd like to know how it feels to stand on a ladder, to peer out and over my rusted pale, just to see how the real world above the 'bucket' lives.

I'd like to know if life pictures me a disorder of an unknown etiology, and like an aphelion thrum, I now exist as an epilogue of a person, lost in the emptiness of a canceled death? Could it have happened this way: someone heard about it from a friend of a friend, or maybe it was told as the gossip of the day at the community hair salon, where everyone drowned in the banquet of delicious food decorating my wake, even helped themselves to another serving or three, and for good measure threw in a few crocodile tears, but in the final analysis someone forgot to mention this fact to me?

I'd like to know what you know.

Do you know how it feels to live each day like a wilted teabag, brewed in the tempered smegma of vegetative mummies, or to pass through life like a dune queen wearing a scorpion crown inherited from a long line of dead women reigning over dusted tumbleweeds and Lysol Basin Tubs and Tile Cleaner?

I wonder if there is enough room for another 'wandering wound' in search of her displaced hymen.

No, just before sleep comes, I always hear something else. It never seems to approach me with the same tone, but when it does come, I am immediately taken to the mouth of the Bluest River where this gnashing deluge of a cynical, wet web awaits. It's not a filthy place, ravaged with scurrying fur balls and long-toothed kin. Neither is it filled with breathtaking breezes, coconut palm trees, golden bananas, and champagne beaches. No, it's not at all like that. This place, in its entire wondrous splendor, somehow, and in some disturbing way, knows me, welcomes me, and calls to me, as if I were commissioned as the Captain of this empty, crewless vessel.

I'd like to know, what is that sound echoing beneath my pillow?

It's not a lulling song, nor do I consider it music. I always thought of it as the billowing raucous of a sandpaper hymn, spewing sickening feelings of buoyant memories, sea stories sung from a restless past with back halls mired in cotton meadows, just south of nowhere, next to a recalcitrant bayou.

Whenever I hear that sound, the ferryman tapping on the door of my ear drummed soul, I am almost always ready to reach way down into the temporal mast of my limbic system and hoist that uncircumcised antenna up by its riveting head and twist and twist, until its honey-dewed, semen-squirting, forget-me-yes days of screwing me up and down, of penetrating my vaginal diaries with his hard songs sung in the key of my shored life, of working my rear as if it were the only ballast available to a ship of fools, of wishing for the day of deepening when he's finally enshrined at the bottom of that graveyard chasm, a circumcised shell, and without a testicular excuse to piss from, for all the gilled ladies to kiss, to peck, to bloat over, forever there, and hung no more, a sunken treasure.

Sigh.

I really would like to know. Am I an impersonal project of the Gods? Perhaps a diminutive experiment personally engineered by untoward Goddesses, the last overturned card invited to their spoiled feast, left wallowing like a maggot along guillotine waterfalls of a diminutive selfdom?

Who stole my primal scream?

Or is there a righteous blessing, no, a horrendously morbid outcome awaiting those like me, who ferry across the River Styx free of charge, to greet those jaded vixens soliciting their labial manuscripts before those East Coast dead-itors and literary wage-ents?

As the years have patiently listened to shadowless echoes questioning my evacuated 'self,' I've learned to listen for other things. I've given up asking sunken-sea questions about things my soul craves but fails to understand. I've given up seeking the normal things in life, because it has yet to believe I exist. I've given up hoping for a half-day of valiance, a moment within someone's Ivory Tower, or merely a chance meeting with Don Quixote, who may be still working his way west – San Francisco – with his lance comfortably ready and his cheeks greased for the tow.

Isn't it funny, though, whenever I'm delivered into the lush and magnificent beauty of this cold, tidal motion, with its intoxicating shrill of illusory Amazonian audience, that I never remember soaring from its horizon, a galley of seagulls or other winged denizens naturally seducing harlotry winds with their erotic lectures and passionate wings? Wouldn't you find it interesting that the only thing I seem to remember when I'm straddling its crest is hearing the call from thrashing waves of an uncompromising River, experiencing nightly the wretched journey to God-knows-where, and then waking before dawn with the word 'albatross' on my mind?

And yet, nightly, the legacy of this tormenting vigil continues to ravage the garden of a sacred vault so crammed with me, so dense with the voice of a wretched phoenix, so unrelenting with its personalized passkey, that I dare not enter upon this vicious path, knighted with the brilliance of an impenetrable forest of humid madness, my dreams.

And try as I might to guild my nightfall with His word, my buckler against branched memories of a deciduous pain, it seems these lofty incursions of meeting them and their ilk, like maggots to flies, are always there, always with me. And never are they without him and that face, his eyes, digging through durable hefty bags I buried deep beneath uncultivated soil within the backyard of my mind. But he did, and he continues to return, nightly, in places I never cared to tread, never dared to open, and, like a spontaneous abortion, never wanted.

But even in the midst of life's entangling webs, even in the hands of the fiercest adversary, and, as I sit here speaking to you from the highest point of my floating galley, like shadows painted with a feather, there remains an answer for me.

For if I am to embrace any more of my night's voyage into another, nakedly bathing in the trenchant Rivers of my braided contempt, ignorantly venturing through an uninterrupted girlish hell with those paradoxical demons and reverberating memories, rafting through that undersea boneyard of resurrected ghouls and coffin-smelling hefty bags, if I am called for another voyage, then I pray for an awakening upstream, where clouds, like salmon, drain across these rivers.

And while the light of mountains parts the water, a Pilate of wind listens to the cock crow thrice, watching my shoreline rise, commanding Aurora.

Tickets, Please

Perilous foreskin

to guide the circumcision

through

relational objects

forgiveness

always tagged

gone

is a trellis of self —

of pulls and tugs

birthing pitch

trailing

for an

weighed

without you

unforgiving grind

undressed mind

Sown Dry

i hate boats
especially   Riverboats
cast   from the sandbar of my concern
adrift

i do not like   sitting   flat
upon a chunk of splintered   mis-erections
floating along   like a rotten piece of driftwood
rocking & reeling   down somebody's stream of dreams
with my stomach   listening to pouting waves
driving up & down my hull   trying to turn me around
with his brainless rudder
veering me from my unspeaking course
wondering   what i'm wondering
hoping   that i hope
knowing that i know
& what for   to catch the driving gale

i do not like   ferries
rising   like Poseidon
steadying   my undertow
steering   me to his flow
saying   'Steady as she goes'
while evanescent clouds   lick the sky
as i   prepare to blow

i do not like   coursing along the dirge of a river
where the shape of things to come
have already dripped & slipped down
          towards the end of the beginning

& why is it when i'm under way he
like a meandrous trickle from   a seafaring penis

flows & sputters   through portly reeds
sung by none other than old man River
when it was known all the while
         he just   keeps rolling along

Caudate Smoke

Whenever light bends, a séance of broken appoggiaturas begin: clouds – swept in an awayness, pasted close to the horizon, and smeared in a foreign color only seen through forgotten windows – linger like viscous smoke borrowing time. With arms akimbo, I stand as a dark fixture lost in a hurricane of brazen words that all too often starts as a whisper and ends with the simmer of a coagulating guillotine. Tales against my body he held like glass before accordion moons, which his earthen chord poured the softest expectations, played my bass curvaceous, walked through a pine of hips, and breathed underwater lotus lips – high low, straight-up jazz, C major. Now, it waxes like neuronal after-discharges, wanes like heavenly starlight licking the speckled face of ponded water.

A cigarette is the only staff unfurling my Red Sea. *Touch me in the morning* – rains through hallways in my crimson mind, along lips that instantly open for the crossing of sacred smoke, down into sarcophagus lungs, forever free, always me, where all of this is exhaled against coronary words still chiming my labia minora and gluteal muscles precisely like a Howard Miller clock – Genesis.

"Why can't you just relax... go with the flow?"

"What do you mean?"

"You know what I damn well mean."

"Well, I try to...but..."

"Stop trying to control every damn thing."

"But I thought we were..."

"Were what?

"You know..."

"How in the hell could you call this...?"

"But we are..."

"Not with you interrupting me."

"What do you mean?

"Look at cha'... always opening your damn mouth, sayin' this and that!"

"But how can I relax with your crude language?

"What the heck that's supposed to mean?"

"...exactly my point."

"Ain't no damn point."

"Look, I said, this is my point."

"Who you think you talking to – a school kid?"

"What?"

"You heard me... I'm tired of your crap."

"Why are you so angry... Ignorant and raw?"

"Angry! Are you kidding?"

"That's what I said."

"If you'd put your nose down, maybe you'd understand why..."

"What does my nose have to do with this conversation?"

"Everything!"

"Then explain it to me, because I don't get it."

"I guess you wouldn't."

"So you're not going to help me understand your point?"

"Hell no!"

"Fine... Then you could at least tell me what's wrong with you."

"*What's wrong with me?* What's right with you?"

"Get off me, nigga...," jerking him out of me.

"Don't you ever push me like that again." He slapped my naked self to the other side of the bed.

Suddenly, I felt the warmth, then the cold plastic feel of an empty milk carton.

"Just when I thought we were moving... in the right direction... as a couple should... and you go and do this!" I said, sniffing and crying.

"Get out of my face..."

"Don't you ever put your hands on me!"

His eyes were as black as his military-shined shoes.

As if he needed to suture the sky, I watched him sow his heading.

The shadow ahead of his stride, the wrinkle in his gait, his shopping bag stuffed with all his clothes, exiting down through long cemented stairs of an old folk's home, towards the Greyhound bus station, ever closer to years stitched with hieroglyphic guilt, false breakthroughs. Strange it was, to see him shovel his feet through a stretch of gravel singing of dust and storm appurtenances, never to return, never to speak, even in another time. Sigh. His melody was so leaf.

Passing subconscious stations chrome as winter, I often wondered if he ever heard Trojan women guiding ribbons across valleys. I also wondered what price this view. But then my only answer has been my need to look out cold windowpanes, where rawhide continues to straddle the noonday mare.

Standing within Marlboro winds always left behind, I exhale sharp passions painted from staccato indigo tides. How interesting it all was, looking out through long-lasting drags, trying to understand when they will cease to orbit dark, female ceilings.

Bullet Proof Soul

Tell me, finally, what is a man? What is a woman? Aren't we lovers first, spirits sharing an uncharted space, a space our stories tell, a space chanted, written upon again and again, yet one story never quite erased by the next, each story saving the space, saving itself, saving us. If someone is listening.
— John Edgar Wideman, *The Cattle Killing* (1992)

2100, Thursday.

Where is Sonia? She knew Sargent had his eyes on her. She knew how difficult he could be when anyone was late for roll call. "Professionalism, a good work ethic, and promptness," he always barked, "go together with our precincts' finest."

I am sure she did not want him docking her pay, again. She knew how difficult he could be when it came to rank and order – stuff that held a greater significance in his day than for our generation today. This Me-Too generation caters to ideas and visions from a universe all their own. Not that I am any wiser, nor am I any older – I'm just thirty years old, mostly.

The wooden bench in our locker room seemed exceptionally hard today. I tried to shift and turn my butt to get a better position, but it was too flat. Butt-naked, I stood up, wondering what it was that I had plastered to my derriere. Nothing new. Just the same ol' hard, flat bench I return to night-in, early-morning out. I shrugged my shoulders, wondering, was it that *that* time already?

"Hey, Elle!" Sonia threw at me, rushing in with her eyelids

stretched to her hairline, gasping for air.

"Well, well, well. Look what the cat drug in."

"What?"

"It's about time, don't you think?"

"What can I say?" rolling her eyes.

"Where you been?"

"What?" stopping dead in her tracks.

"Do you know what time it is?"

"Oh, that..."

"It seems you love living dangerously?"

"Yeah, sometimes I wonder about that..."

"Don't we all?"

"So, how's your gorgeous husband?" she asked.

"Girl, he's always complaining about my working too much... never home to help out with our son."

"Why hasn't he left you yet?"

"And how many knuckle-dragging prostates did you suck this weekend?

"Oh, and on which street corner did you leave your pair of wet panties?"

Sonia laughed so hard her face nearly kissed her knees.

"It's so nice to see you, too," I said, flashing my much-better-looking pearl whites.

Eight years earlier, fresh out of the police academy, Sonia and I first met, and here we remain, prisoners to the broken heart of Amygdala Blue, a city we often say we fell from, as new recruits to the 47th Precinct.

Here, we rise every night, like vampires with a badge, serving all manner of murderers, criminals, blood-drained victims. Unlike the undead, we prey on the unjust, miscreants lacking a conscience, diseased citizens whose blood remains tainted from birth, and probably until death.

For a thirty-five-year-old Black woman, Sonia was not bad looking – smooth, brown, clean complexion, shoulder-length natural hair, and clear, sober eyes. Despite my henna-rooted hair, my hazel-green eyes, even with my Carnation-milk complexion and medium-build frame, I still was no match for her feminine wiles. Her mantel of a butt always made me look twice at the absence of mine. I hated her for that.

Sonia and I were hard workers, two of Amygdala Blue's finest police officers. After eight years, we finally earned our reputations as "some of the guys" at the 47th Police Precinct. We were the only two women who could handle revolvers just as easily as any Dick patrolling the streets of Amygdala Blue. What Dicks they all were. Not one of them could juggle their personal lives as well as they claimed to wield their penises. The truth was that our colleagues were good partners, but lousy husbands, boyfriends, significant others, whatever you wish to call someone of the opposite sex who wanted nothing other than that. In truth, all of them was worthless whore-hounds. Sonia often referred to them as "Cop-less" men..." Just one minute away from the force, and the next thing you know, they are in-between another pair of legs... or two.

"Did you hear about the new recruits?" Sonia said, strapping her bulletproof vest around her coke-bottle waistline and firm breasts.

"No, I didn't," struggling to zip up my pants. "Uhm..."

"I heard new recruits are scheduled to arrive next weekend."

"Well, it's about time..."

"You're telling me."

"We certainly could use the help around here. With the rise in unemployment, this city seems to fall deeper into darkness," she said, bending down to tie up her tight, leather-bound boots.

"Well, I don't know 'bout you, but I'm tired of working 'round-the-clock shifts."

"Me too..."

"How many recruits are we talking?"

"I don't know exactly. Probably five to seven..."

"Really?"

"I kid you not."

"Well, barring their training period, anything still beats our crazy shifts."

"Hear, hear."

"Are you working tomorrow night?"

"It just so happens, I'm off. And you?"

"I have to work."

The next night's shift proceeded like no other. Halfway through the drudging of paperwork and inventory and schedule maintenance, I received a call about a domestic dispute involving an unusual couple known to everyone in the 47th. I remembered one time, the husband busted the wife's lip and blacked both her eyes. The next time, she caught him from behind, and cracked his head with a hammer, or maybe it was a baseball bat. Blood was everywhere! Just when we thought we had seen it all, even after locking one of them up, like clockwork, the spouse showed up with bail money to initiate round two, sometimes round three. "It's always what *you* want, never enough, never. When are you going to understand, the world does not revolve around *your* needs? When...!" I heard him say, as they exploded out the precinct onto the street. There she was, pounding his ear, "What do you mean? You lazy son of a ..."

In the car on our way to their address, my partner Sam kept his hands locked on the steering wheel. He did not say much, but I saw him shaking his head, probably wondering why this couple could not get it together. For a moment, I wondered if he saw me doing the same. As we drove up to their home, I could tell something was not quite right. The front door was wide open. Light from the inside poured onto the front porch – the curtains were wide open, no one in sight.

The air smelled sweet like a mayonnaise sandwich. Crickets took center stage, serenading the night. Off to my right, I saw my partner signal he had the left side of the home. Another officer, with shotgun clenched, rose from his crouching stance and approached from the other side. Gripping my trusty revolver, I proceeded up the middle. Carefully, quietly, cautiously.

On the count of three, we rushed the house. Within a second we stood in the living room. Everything around us lay in a disordered silence. Furniture was broken, curtains hung like weeping willows, dishes and glass lay shattered along the dingy brown carpet and bare floor, and just a few feet away, their 17" television lay on its side, smashed in. Turning around, I found the husband drenched in beaded specks of blood and dirt, naked. He was a tall black man. Odd it was, that I noticed his long, thick legs. I followed the husband's eyes, fixed on the broken coffee table where his wife's body lay peacefully in death. Curled in his right hand, he held a broken leg from a dining room chair that dripped with her blood. It was not hard to miss the wife's nearly decapitated head as it lay half torn from her neck, her blood soaking the rug.

He was a mess! Everything around him mirrored their struggle, the last remaining vestige of what *was* their marriage, their vows. I wondered what ran through his mind, as he stood gazing at his dead wife. I wondered if had his mind with him. Moreover, I wondered about mysterious underpinnings driving human nature. He never moved, didn't recognize us, even when we circled in front of him with our guns drawn, ready.

The sound he made when he breathed was loud and eerie. It was almost as if we could hear him wheeling his breath through the wind tunnel of his homicidal mind. It sounded like a rusted bicycle tire. His face, his horribly scarred face, was vacant. He appeared locked in a homicidal stupor to which no consciousness had yet returned. I felt my arms lower, my mind and stomach sick with disgust, rage, horror to the ninth power. I felt a sudden urge to unload all my gun's bullets into his head, what was left of his soul.

He did not attempt to flee, and he did not seem surprised by our presence. He just stood there with stark eyes, probably frozen in his final attempt at reconciliation. I felt a powerful temptation to poke my finger into his eye. Sam shook his head. I agreed that the husband was not all there. With my mind revolving, I looked long and hard at their shambled surroundings, what was left of their home. I quickly broke away, stepped back to take a good frontal view at him, his long dangling piece. That thing gave me goosebumps, his limp snake. I looked at the swirling vein sitting atop his manhood. I thought about its feeling. For a moment, a good female moment, I wandered through a subconscious garden painted in the desire of a forceful waterfall. For a moment, I swam its shore brilliantly.

Wait a minute, I thought, something was wrong. Why was it bleeding? There was lots of blood pouring down upon the floor... The head of his penis was missing! Yet, he seemed completely numb to it all. How could he withstand such pain? Where was it?

"Look around for the rest of his dick!" I yelled at Sam. A few feet away, I could hear him stumbling like a child refusing to go to bed. He was always funny that way, taking directions from a female, but I outranked him. I just shook my head. We dug through their wreckage for nearly ten minutes, before, yes, my god! I found it. No, oh my God, no! There, inside the mouth of his dead wife, we found a clump of thick meat stewing in a soup of saliva, semen, and blood.

---

4 AM.

No Starbucks cup of coffee, no Crispy Crème donuts could settle my nerves. I was like smoldering embers, nearly spent. The stress of working the graveyard shift, coupled with the spousal homicide, was enough to snap the strongest spine in two. I needed a break from the insanity of this city's ever-increasing rate of homicidal indiscretions and senseless felonies. I needed to see my husband and son, touch home base for some psychological relief. I needed to go somewhere safe, *normal*. I needed a hug.

One more minute of that precinct and I would go nuts, literally. Initially, bound to protocol, Sargent utterly refused. Then he eventually gave in to my urgings and decided to let me go home early. "Go on, just get outa here!" he barked with a smile. Thank God, because I had enough.

I was so tired that I let my weary body slump into the front seat of my eight-year-old Honda Accord. Riding along, I let my body hang deep into the comfortable crux of my car's smelly aroma that cupped the edge of my butt like water in a glass. Next thing I knew, Sade's soulful rhythms of "Bullet Proof Soul" serenaded me as I glided through dark, whispering neighborhoods, long concrete tongues of streets speaking of a lukewarm loneliness, where tin-can noses smelled of back-alley despair and aged light beams drooled upon front porch droppings.

I always believed this was where the eyes joined the ears for listening, eyes lost in the dance and kiss of pantomime shadows. Here is where singing fingers issue forth as a roll of thunder. Here, amid a knowing community, is where shadows deal in whispers. For darkness has sacred power, a deadly voluptuousness served to us all. It is within the deepest part of darkness that suffering dwells, hungry for another, the deepest part of night in which the nape of desire thrives. Vampires, I tell you. That is all we are, hedonistic vampires always in search of--

I couldn't resist the urge to repeat Sade's "Bullet Proof Soul" as the steering wheel wiggled and turned, steered – it knows the way home. Thoughts surrounding that poor unfortunate couple continued to invade my mind – his face, their matrimonial outcome, what we found in her mouth – all of it made me feel completely lunar, as if I were lost in the pit of a countryside well. Like tongue to mouth, the memory of the wife's death hugged tight my sanity. I thought about how devastating it was to languish in a cauldron of despair, to wander corrosive corridors leading nowhere. How could such a thing happen? Are we nothing more than slaves to the paradisiacal elixir of choices? The answers continued to evade me like cars I passed along dark, hapless boulevards, completely without the capacity to sleep, afraid to weep.

This time of morning, even the crickets knew slumber. No one really cared about enacting a crime at dawn. It was too early in the morning. It was against the nature of man, against the laws of the universe for anyone to think of such a thing. Tired, disgusted, I lifted myself up and out of my trusted vehicle, which knew probably more about me than my husband. Strange, the kitchen door was unlocked. A few of the lights were still on. I looked about the kitchen, checked the sink, and peered into the living room, the dining room. No one was there. Everything seemed to be in order.

My first act upon arriving home is always to remove my shoes. I must relieve my feet of garish leather boots, revive the circulation to feet screaming to breathe. I sat for a moment to massage the middle of my arch, my ankles, and my spoiled toes. What an orgasmic relief, plopping down on the edge of the sofa, leaning back on the comfort of familiar pillows. I let the moment wash over me, gently, pleasingly – the joy of silence, the serenity of *home*, sanctuary, absolute medicine for the soul. Then I heard noises, strange sounds. Suddenly, my smile fell away, my back arched. I looked around again. A mist of wine and roses hung in the air like the sanguineous gong from a temple bell. A faint eerie feeling began in the lower portion of my stomach. Perhaps my imagination, running rampant from the night's horrific events.

I started upstairs, my feet taking each step slowly. When I got to the top of the stairs, I peeped into our son's room. My son Jason was lying comfortably on his back, fast asleep. His breathing echoed throughout his tiny, toy-filled room. Reassured, I smiled. Then I heard that noise again. It was not in here. Curious, I crept back into the hall, stood for a moment, and walked towards our bedroom. There, I found the bedroom door half-opened. The light was on. Its glow struck like a blues piano song tickling along.

Richard was in bed, and not at all alone. As if there was an x-ray apron resting on my chest, I struggled to catch my breath, I barely remained conscious to endure the nasty taste of bile in my mouth.

"...you fucking BASTARD!" I thought came from my mouth.

Suddenly their ride beneath the sheets came to a sudden halt. Up from their bedded garden they sprang – their odors reeked of GUILTY!

Like an old man lost in a dream too close to the death of a fantasy, Richard looked at me with a vacant grin, speechless. With hair unkempt, lipstick smudged along the outer edges of her nose, jaw, and chin like a Picasso painting, Sonia jumped, turned around, revealing exhausted bite-marked nipples. In between the inner sanctum of my heart-beating eardrums, the tearing of neurons sounded. It was as if nerves along the inside of my spinal cord had been ripped away, one segment at a time.

"Get out of my bed, BITCH!"

As if Sonia took umbrage to my discovery, she snatched the sheet up to her neckline. Disdain sat on her face like a flag wrestling with deep winds. Her complexion had taken on a darker shade. I saw points along the corner of her mouth draw in like prunes, while her eyes hissed and spit hatred.

I barely remember how their slow, grudging scent poured through the buxom air like mist from Eden, penitential, palpable. I barely remember seeing various articles of Egyptian cotton accessorizing the floor and bed. Surely, I cannot say I remember grabbing the holster from my shoulder and palming my weapon tightly. No, I do not. What I do remember, though, is how Sonia aimed her deep brown eyes squarely into mine, and without an ounce of visible remorse or shame, challenged me with her razor-sharp stare. Standing there, barely able to hear my mind, I felt the grating edge of her feminine daggers. I felt her pride and shame parading through me, kicking like a child at the height of a tantrum. With every passing second, her stare spoke daringly from the marrow of her desire to strike and take what bit of *him* she believed was hers, had always been hers!

Like lead crystal-pinged by a fingernail, the edge of my womanhood chimed unendingly to a song playing for an endangered species. The acoustics were as beautiful as a Philharmonic symphony, as forceful as childbirth. I felt a nimbus of rage wash over me, and so it was that Sonia received my fervent reply –

––––––––

"Honey... I... I... can explain. L-let... let me explain!"

"Explain what, husband?" I said, pointing my smoking .38 revolver three feet away from the center of his eyes. The heavy line of tears stopped just at the base of my chin, now icicles leaping into the fray.

"Honey, you... you... you don't know what... you're doing."

"Oh, I know what I'm doing."

"No... honey, please!"

"Do you, my beloved, know what you've done?"

"Honey... let me... have the gun. Please, give me the gun..."

"You fucked our vows ... with Sonia!"

"No, honey..."

"How many times have we discussed this? Never FUCK our vows!"

"Honey, I didn't mean..."

"Of course, you didn't mean to."

I felt a dark smile forming on my face. Frantically, he reached out to me like a puppy, tears flowing down the sides of his pitiful face, his lower lip quivering.

"Please honey, don't... I love you."

"Do you *truly* remember those sacred words? Do you remember?" I slammed the gun across his face. "Do you?"

His head lowered, crying.

"Repeat after me, you vile piece of bacteria..."

"I... can't..."

"Say it! For richer or poorer..."

"Honey, listen to me."

"Till death do we part," I moved in closer.

"Please honey… no!"

Everything became a theatre as I saw myself – or someone who looked exactly like me, dressed like me, broken like me, pissed off like me – take to the stage in the lead role, confidently in character, raising the gun…

"Mommy…Daddy." Still in his flannel Pokémon pajamas, our four-year-old son Jason strolled in rubbing sleep from his eyes.

"No, Jason, don't come any closer, stay over there."

"Jason, come to Daddy," Richard interrupted.

"No, Jason!"

Unknowingly, Jason chose the waiting arms of his father ,who snatched him up like a blanket thrown to a naked man standing barefoot in the snow.

"Let him go, Richard."

"Put the gun down Eleanor," his face now alive with intentional feeling, bargaining power. Suddenly, I thought of the many felons, thieves, and thugs I had arrested, sometimes interrogated, frequently escorted to prison. His heart was truly terrible, now beating mine to a pulp.

"Mommy…"

I started to quiver, the inside of my gut knotting up.

"It's alright baby…Mommy's right here." I threw up my arm to reassure him everything was all right.

"That's right Jason, Mommy is right here, and she will DO the right thing. Won't you Mommy?"

"Richard, you low-life scum, put our son down, now!" My gun remained pointed at his chest.

"Put the gun down, Eleanor, and I'll let our son go…"

Completely naked, but refusing to budge, Richard shielded himself behind Jason's small torso. His eyes burned with the cavernous stare of a raven. His mouth filled with a desperation that began to slowly dry as he slyly inched towards the bedroom door. But I was closer than he; in fact, I was standing just in front of it, determined.

As if he had forgotten about what had initiated all of this, Richard took a moment to look at Jason's expression. As the moment progressed and the heat of the struggle continued, I somehow became the jury lead standing at the edge of the jury box with paper in hand, and ready to announce the verdict. How all this transpired, I have not a clue.

Suddenly I saw the gun discharge its fatal content into the air, release a rippling verdict of uncompromising justice. My hand felt its powerful expression. A frightening delay numbed my sense of hearing, rocked my perceptive reasoning. I saw the bullet barreling along, pushing through forested molecules and vapors and damning ions like a foot slamming a roach into the cold, unforgiving pavement. I craned forward, my mind fully in flight. When I did hear it seconds later, it came as a sheer tone of intransigent truth. As if a catcher's mitt poised for the long high fly ball to drop, Richard's forehead accepted the empurpled bullet squarely between his eyes. I watched him settle to the hard floor as stagnant dust, listless, forgotten like a man returning to his lost boyhood. I watched as Jason rolled away from his arms breathing and whining, frightened but completely unharmed.

"Daddy…"

"It's okay, honey," I said, dropping the gun, nearly constricting Jason in my arms.

For a long moment, we stood in the middle of the floor, locked in each other's arms, our heartbeats as one.

Even with my eyes shut, the hellacious symphony continued to reel in my mind, reverberating through the lightshow nailed to my eardrums. I wanted it all to cease, I wanted it all to go away, but it was not possible. There were no commercials, there was no intermission, this performance was not about to be canceled. This show had top billing, and *I* was its star.

"Mommy, who is that lady?" pointing his little finger over to where the body of Sonia lay.

For a quick moment, I glanced at Sonia, lying face down in a pool of blood. Although justice prevailed – my justice – the sinewy thread upholding my reason broke. Its connection with reality was utterly broken. Upon my mind's canvas, an obsessive beat played. Although beautiful in harmony, I saw myself plunging ever lower into the garden of the abyss, smelling every aspect of a landscape blossoming with graves, every path frothing with romantic auras, tasting the cracked marrow of prosecuted bones.

"Mommy, why you pee on the floor?" Jason asked, his wide eyes glaringly pure, beseeching me to come back, stay with him. "You not supposed to go potty on yourself."

I wanted to look at him, to take him into parts of me still alive. I wanted to say something that only a mother can communicate to her child, but–

"Mommy, your eyes..."

His voice was so soft, so pure, fleeting.

"Mommy, what's wrong with your face?"

Out into the velvet prism, kaleidoscopically so true, I look straight through him as a whirl of sirens whine ever closer to an Amygdala Blue truth. Even as this song played on early morning violins that arrested my soul, I fell into the sharp scallops of my favorite Sade song – "Bullet Proof Soul" – that patrolled long corridors decorated with the fragrance of fresh vows, desperately clinging to the lyrics of my soul.

These were tears I heard raining down upon every city, I heard feelingly, as the gun inched closer toward the face of my left temple.

"No mommy, don't!" is what I remember hearing last...

Enduring Oath

I sat on the edge of my bed, sheets awry, cradling both sides of my face as I listened to my mind's playback of our enduring conversation:

"So, the whole idea," I said, "behind the picnic at your house, was to...".

"Go ahead, say it."

"... and Dr. Shorter had no idea?"

"And why would he?"

"I mean–"

"Yes, I know what you mean."

"But how could he not know?"

"Simple. He loves me."

I looked at her for what seemed like hours but was only a minute and said, "How long has this been going on?"

"C'mon," she said, "let's enjoy the time we have."

"Wow, you say that with a great deal of expectation."

"That depends on you," Evelyn said.

"Well...," I said, wondering how I would reconcile the notion that Dr. Jerome Bartholomew Shorter – Medical Director of John Hopkins University's Department of Internal Medicine – was her husband and my boss.

With lips soft as lilies, wet with the inscription of morning dew, Evelyn Shorter was as driven as a Sahara sand dune. At forty years of age, she was the epitome of an erotic professor, always lecturing, eager to teach her twenty-five-year-old medical resident – *me* – anatomy and physiology techniques via braille.

Her intimate wasteland, savage and free, reminded me of wind sweeping rain, seething with breath, unbridled morning flesh. Whenever we made love, our pulses raged from the kitchen table to the stairwell, the backyard swing to the bulky dryer, from the stale air perfuming their Victorian attic to *their* lavish countryside bedroom. All of this we clandestinely tasted without manners needed for fine China, our primitive meal served deliciously sweet and raw.

During clinical rounds the next day, I suffered through the grandeur of her mulatto fragrance still engrained upon the pad of my tongue. Can you imagine my feeling when my elderly patient caught sight of the bulge in my pants, then stared especially hard at my embarrassing smile? Could my face turn any redder? I needed to get a breath of fresh air, get a grip on my thoughts, only to return for another patient, always there, always waiting. Who was I kidding? Second-Year internal medicine residents do not have time for such things. These pleasures remain the cornerstone of experiences handed over to writers, artists, the bulk of rural communities, I thought, walking past the nurse's station to view the next patient's chart, shaking my head, all the while smiling.

Several weeks later, it became abundantly clear I unknowingly had become addicted to a drug Evelyn notoriously loved to peddle over the counter. Every fix was as divine as the first time, every dose as hedonistically debilitating as the next. However true it was for any man who dabbled in things known to strip away one's inner self, I was addicted to her. Frequently, I was compelled to bother my staff and nurses with the need to reschedule patients, out somewhere with Evelyn, she all over me, me reciprocating, and surprisingly nothing was made of it. Deep into the night, when I lay across my bed alone, thoughts foreign to the whole of this wondrous experience began to slither into my mind, invading my pleasure principle with doubting questions. I needed to know...

"I was wondering..."

"Wondering what?" Evelyn said.

"Well, you know..."

"How many young medical residents have I been with?"

"No, I mean... Well, yes."

As if she anticipated the question, had done this before, she took the time, an experienced amount of time, and then with the utmost confidence of a lioness resting under a tree, she rolled her Elizabeth Taylor eyes with *Cleopatra* poise. I watched her sit up, tilt her head coyly to one side, slowly stroll her well-manicured nails through her chestnut kingdom of hair.

Phenotypically, Evelyn was a cross between an 'MGM' Lena Horne and Beyoncé Knowles. Suddenly, I thought about her compositional DNA. What a powerful concept, at least from my eye's perspective – nature's powerful ability to add cocoa to one's vanilla, or just a little cream in one's coffee. I thought about the meaning of 'race.' I thought about how postmodern civilized societies are wrong, a simple thing as listening to the rhythm of forests, harmony bristling beneath nature's skirt, living as a song that plays throughout like a symphony celebrating life, the whole universe. I felt my eyes roll up towards her forehead, examining the base of her hairline, roots speaking with little tiny specks of grey. Up close, glimmers of age danced just beneath her caramel epidermal layer. The thought of genetic drift almost took my mind off my primary query, the real purpose for our discussion.

"I was wondering when you'd get around to asking about my prior escapades, my extramarital adventures."

I could feel my jaw muscles tighten.

"As you may well imagine, with you being a doctor and all, yes, you are not my first; maybe my fifth, or my sixth? I can't remember," she laughed. "But you're probably wondering why I would need to do such a thing, given that I am married to Dr. Jerome Bartholomew Shorter, your boss."

The mention of his name cut into the firmness of my wood. I heard a tree fall quietly in the forest. She looked down briefly, then back to me.

"Everything in life is centered around desire and need and how to sustain it, because you never know when it might run dry. The longer you have it, the better off you are."

She did not blink. The song from her story knew no intermezzo as it rang with a burning truth. I wondered if I had struck a nerve, or was her reply merely a subconscious justification for a peaceful sleep lying next to *him*?

"This notion of need cuts like a double-edged sword. Nothing in this world is perfect. Not me, my husband, certainly not the logic of

God. Therefore, when it comes to a women's need for power, security, genuine love – constantly – isn't it obvious to ask, 'why should we behave any differently?'

"The bottom line is that my husband is a short-dick, passionless intellectual who sleeps in my bed because *he* has the financial means to provide for my peculiar habits. As you no doubt know, I have a voracious appetite for all things appealing to the senses, including things found in shopping malls, cluttering the internet, and of course, my one-million-dollar home, complete with the 2022 EQS 450+ Mercedes Benz. What more could a girl ask of a man, if his flaws include a weakness in his pants and an insatiable addiction to work?"

"So, the reason why you chose me…?"

"Yes, he has no dick, and if he did I'm convinced he still wouldn't know what to do with it, at least not with me anyway. Can you imagine, a black man without a dick? What has this world come to?"

Her eyes smacked mine with a hard stare. Like the intensity of rage immediately following the act of homicide, her confidence was powerful.

"Haven't you and he discussed this problem before? I mean, talked about alternatives?" I asked.

"Of course, we have. Look, talk, talk, talk, I am tired of talking with someone like him. He is a doctor, a man of his professional stature is quite accustomed to having things done his way; used to telling people what to do, and not the other way around. Come on, Dr. Given, you know what I mean."

Even though she was right, I was not about to let her know the male ego is like Mount Everest, well-formed and full of it.

"But doesn't he know…?"

"Know that I am an *attractive* woman? That I have a mind, that I have *needs*? Why do you think *he* married me?"

"But doesn't he suspect that you…?"

"Suspect that I engineered his yearly internist residency picnic at our house so that I can survey the incoming young, virulent, good-looking males? Of course not…"

Suddenly, I wondered how it was that so many men could be so successful in their careers, yet at home with the little woman, via the power of the vagina, the reigns to his kingdom dramatically, ironically shifts hands. Could this very notion exist as a sub-punishment to our eviction from the Garden of Eden, not to mention the loss of our rib? Was this a part of God's plan, penance for succumbing to the temptation of a delicious bite, uxoriously, for a heinous crime – the disobedience of His most cherished command – to forever thirst after and be completely blinded by a skirt, lips that speak a dangerously sweet elixir? For some strange reason, this thought took a gripping hold of me, and I was left dangling like drooping balls.

"Jerome and I have been married since I was twenty years old. What an incredulous notion – me, married nearly twenty years."

Like a smoker badly in need of a fix, she licked her lips. The aperture on my lens tried to zero in closer, but all I could see was her head nodding and the door to her heart hermetically sealed. I wanted to knock, but I knew she was the type who opened her intrapersonal door rarely.

"Have you ever been married?" pushing the cover away from her rapturous body to put on a robe. "Of course, you haven't...

"Let me tell you something, don't forget about love, but whatever you do, dismiss any notion of marriage. This is a vile concept designed for *dreamers*. A long time ago, I was one such person who invested the whole of my essence into this dream of doom – marriage!

"Believe me when I say this: today, all marriages are doomed to fail. This is the reason why I do not have any girlfriends with whom I can sit and have a genuine conversation, not as men do. With women, it is impossible. Women always need a man. Now that is what I call an *eternal sin* – always needing somebody, yearning for him like the next breath. Why, when there's the world of available bodies to have at your beck and call, to taste whenever you need to, like going to the refrigerator and pulling out a carton of milk and lifting it right up to your lips and drowning in its sweetness – cold and nourishing, yours for the tasting."

Oh, how this Sabre of truth can be so swift in exposing the undercurrent of our lifeblood. Something seemed terribly wrong with her tone, the way she let fly her sharp, bowel-emptying speech, not just about her husband, but all men. The more I looked at her, the more I wanted to believe how diseased this concept of man and woman seemed. How pathological it appeared in the sight of a nature that lacked any serious sense of humor. I began to wonder if a woman's need for a man existed merely to learn how to dominate him, dethrone his masculinity sanctioned long ago in the Garden of Eden, to conquer his nature. The strategy laid in this social middle game went way beyond the natural order of history – now *her-story*.

———

Outside Dr. Shorter's office, dressed in a stained white coat, nametag tilted, pockets filled with notes and several pens, I sat on a wooden bench, waiting for my appointment. How uncomfortable it was, a doctor waiting for another doctor. How funny to think of such a thing. Would God ever have to wait for another? Of course not: Thou shall have no other gods before me. On the other hand, was I confusing my reasoning with 'Till death do we part'?

Upon my face, the weight of a fractured self, stuck like swamp mud. I felt forlorn, wondered if my deodorant failed. On the faces of people passing by, I saw loud expressions of distastefulness, eyes reflecting scenes of me carrying a mop and bucket. I saw myself drowning during a guillotine light – a place morally running from Dante.

Thirteen minutes past 10:30 am, thirteen minutes after Evelyn's thirteenth message on my pager, Dr. Shorter's door opened. He greeted me with an expression as if I were a patient in need of a diagnosis. For a moment, my mind spun differentially.

"Dr. Given. How are you?" Dr. Shorter said, with a contrived air of respect.

"Hello, Dr. Shorter. Well, thank you."

"Good," he said shaking my hand firmly. "Please come in and have a seat."

"Thank you, sir."

Dr. Shorter took a few minutes to clear a few items from the paper storm swirling about his desk. As I had already surmised, he was quite the busy person. I did not mind waiting. I was not too anxious to begin talking, so the longer he took, the better it probably was for the both of us.

Laden across his polished mahogany desk were stacks of *New*

England Journal of Medicine, BMJ, Lancet, JAMA, and *American Journal of Surgery* journals. Against the wall, adjacent to the view of a bustling sophomoric campus, there was a bicycle. Dry mud was stuck to its tires, the spokes were somewhat warped, the seat was torn, handlebars drooped, and the chain was caked with a dark, oily substance. Whose was it? For the life of me, I could not believe it was his, or he even took the time to consider riding it. I do not know why I felt this way; perhaps it had something to do with my extracurricular influence.

"So, how are Grand Rounds coming?"

The light coming from his window splashed upon me as if I were on stage, about to render the performance of a lifetime. I could but hope that I would not disappoint the audience, maybe forget my lines.

"Just fine, thank you. Indeed, there are many patients in the Internal Medicine outpatient clinic these days with very special needs. Epidemiologically speaking though, atherosclerosis and familial hypertension seem to be on the rise."

"Good work. Our biostatisticians have verified this to be a concern."

"And the nurses?"

"What nurses? Don't you mean the lack thereof?"

We both laughed, briefly.

"Yes, Evelyn – you know, my wife – she thought you might stop by," with arms akimbo, a stolid smile hung beneath a fenced hello.

"So, Dr. Given, what's on your mind?"

Hippocampal Lash

Upon my shoulder, like handkerchief to lips, struggling to wipe the moment clean – it laid an improbable cause, real. Neither a mirror abetted with smoke, nor a magnifying glass squarely tucked between two cheeks, lying. This was no fata morgana. No, this looking-glass wonderland didn't need Alice. Nor did it dream Snow White. Instead, it got the whole of my narrative, my reasoning, my gonfalon, my wife, even the seed of my grandchildren. Everything of mine it had to govern into the red of an Amygdala-Blue. Well-versed in the fluency of bled gold running like hot knife to buttered soul, my impetus took court – spoke before a solstice Come-Monday. Do you believe the love of art is truly the extinction of personality? No other reason is due. Perhaps a political concept thrown before wolves. But wolves and philosopher-poets seldom mix. Except in the jaws of scorn, saliva regurgitated for the pure... marginalized... told you aren't worthy of a community, foul beneath fowl, gifted with an aquiline feature whores would demand a price for three. That the naked truth being the personality of art is but gestalt on steroids, forever unrealized; addicted to a cursed eternity, lived as an intangible kernel screaming–

I need more!

Although Short & Sensitive

Although short & sensitive   we dick
in the bowl of sapphire memories   wormwood songs
blood boiling over   like coagulated orchids
waiting for our proboscis   to sticky lick its solar sweet
pollinate beyond

Although short & sensitive   we stand
in hourglass slammerkins   guilelessly worn like therapeutic togas
spitting earth wind & broken fire

Don't speak to us   about our Nicki Hill gyri
storming down   sharp & slow-wave catwalks
No revelations about   sacred diseases—
          Dostoevsky: Julius Caesar: Mozart: Napoleon: Socrates:
paraded as complex partial shells

Instead   we ask
speak about astrocytic salt—
          Black Beauty: Cocaine: Crack: Meth: Oxycodone:
shaking us up & out   from Purple Haze   me-too throbs

Although short & sensitive   we awake
          dripping   drooling   drowning
nearly immured   possibly halved
wailing from our   yellow-brick heaven
we still hear   Billie Holiday songs
          cursing   the silence declined

Faces

oak branches reach

through villages   veiled

beneath nuoc mam frowns—

enlightened cracks   creak

above unwilling spills

leaving

       every chào buổi sáng

     every gaze

           very little

Sir, Yes Sir

& there was never any toilet paper
never any soap   not even a blanket
                                              just salivary glands
washing up against   underarm hopes

& yesterday   eye had a sore throat
dry as hashish
salty as the Dead Sea
& from my ass
chickens continue to fall
like spent shells
cracking the red   green chickadees

& today   eye shot around
looking for   regurgitated sweat glands
while
                Monday
                Wednesday
                Friday
                every Sunday

                                              eye bury rubber thalami
deep behind thick lips asking
When will the chopper arrive?

This was metabolized as a journey
never ridden with a smile as
                                              eye digest what's left in my boots
scraps from blue potatoes in my underwear
minister to seasons—

crucifying Charlie
rebuking Snoopy
backsliding Lucy

& tomorrow
before a billion points of aortic lights
cast across a faceless velvet canvass   twirling
with 7 spleens ducking & diving   whirling
                                                                        eye watch Mars

salute every Corporal
yelling with every breath

                                            eye followed my orders...!

Furious Flowers

When sirens scrape the rocky red light of day

an enigmatic ocean glistens with purpose

old orgy   must sea ––

While wavelengths cycle & crash

blue peaks: green troughs: purple bases:

trident vapors on the half-shell

slip down   sloping seaways ––

Lost rainbows   ragamuffins

Georgia muffins: bagels: Buffalo Soldier bread:

lost lugging abortions & broken tongues & misbegotten glands

& scattered flesh & questioning wood & sunken pasts

fettered to Old-Testament straw & mud & mule-bone bricks

smelling of a 60-minute lash   we rise

Lost in every limbic wash   we walk

(leaking urine from seaweed veins)

     to touch Lame Deer palms

     to feel the smooth skin flowering back

     to taste the buffalo-calf-bone pipe

hoping to find the eagle & ghost dance

Lost as a midrib   we turn

in search of our mother's leaves   languishing

between trampled   Native American moccasins

lingering   Auschwitz ash

The Unborn Salt

Half of the fellow father as he doubles

His sea-sucked Adam in the hollow hulk,

Half of the fellow mother as she dabbles

To-morrow's diver in her horny milk,

Bisected shadows on the thunder's bone

Bolt for the salt unborn.

The fellow half was frozen as it bubbled

Corrosive spring out of the iceberg's crop,

The fellow seed and shadows as it babbled

The spring of milk was tufted in the pap,

For half of love was planted in the lost,

And the unplanted ghost.

– Dylan Thomas, *My World Is Pyramid*

"All rise."

With forehead glistening, black robe swaying, peeping over a small pair of glasses that hung low on his sharp nose, Judge Harold B. Alright pushed into his courtroom. As he plopped down on his leatherback throne, he quickly glanced at the defendant, then out into a sea of eyes. Under his robe, he felt like a dishrag in a kitchen run by homeless people. When will the spills and broken dishware cease? But then, he reasoned, was it truly possible to clean society of its uncivil-ized natives, their thirst for roaches?

———————

Hennessey Brown sat on the end of a wooden bench, alone. Although his tailored blue suit gave him the appearance of a recent graduate from an Ivy League university, although he had skin as glossy as a wintry night, although he was not a defendant this time, he was still an invisible man.

Not unlike the finest taste of cognac, Hennessey was exceptionally smooth in character, and long in the mouth. This never really mattered to him. Neither nervousness nor prayers were part of his thirty-two-year-old outtake on life. He was not sitting there today, nor throughout all of the court's proceedings, to learn about the federal judicial system. No. This, he knew all too well.

Hennessey Brown sat on the end of a long bench of small and large shoulders, foreign body odors, conflicting perfumes, nervous knees, rapid breathes, hands wringing, and all sorts of fearful auras, with a specific strategy in mind. There was much to gain from the art of silence, the experience of timing. To him, spiders and snakes were best in the game of life and death, lieutenants of natural darkness, lords of the ultimate game of survival. They knew how to adapt, evolve – to stay two steps ahead of the herbivorous lot. Hennessey wasn't in the least educated, barely made it out of junior high school, but by virtue of his cunning abilities, he would be spared society's scourge. Such was Hennessey: an anomaly, a male Black Widow spider.

Today, Hennessey sat in court to hear "our Country tis' of thee..." spew its constitutional laws upon one of its finest citizens – his wife – a defendant against the State. This is what mattered to Hennessey Brown because he loved *this* country, America. Only in America could such a thing happen. Only in America should this ever happen, he smiled. And so he watched patiently as the wheels of justice churned slowly.

———————

With silky blonde hair, glaring blue eyes, and swollen feet, Noelene Livingston-Brown sat uncomfortably in a chair especially reserved for her. The chair was too hard, her back ached, and her breasts were naturally full. Thirty years old, she was a docket number sensationalized before the highest court for allegedly violating one of God's most sacred commandments: Thou Shall Not Kill.

Behind the passing of the bailiff's shadow, Judge Alright scanned the audience, and then he gave a nod. The bailiff continued towards the door marked "Private," tapped with a light code, and stood with big, scaly, ashy hands folded over his belly. Noelene watched the bailiff and Judge with a subdued interest. In her mind, it seemed as if the chatter swelling in the enveloping heat seemed sublimated. Open only to the capriciousness of another space and time, she felt like a tender thought standing on the insemination of a vortex where she witnessed everyone, including herself in this free-floating consciousness. So free, so pure, so neonatal. There, she continued to float in its vast sea of whiteness, intoxicated with an everlasting shoreline of breaking waves, flamingos, zephyrs, forever forgiving, forever...

With a slight turn of the door handle, the bailiff grabbed everyone's attention. Like soldiers, in walked the chosen twelve – eight women, four men (three African Americans, seven Caucasians, two Hispanics) – one by one, and in single file. The long expressions on their faces hung like paraffin wax nearing its boiling point. Each juror appeared careful to evade eye-to-eye contact, to lock away any indication of the final verdict. But they could taste the crowd's curiosity, hijacking the air like metal to the tongue. They could feel the electricity of the audience.

"Has the jury reached a verdict?" the Judge roared.

"Yes, your honor, we have."

Noelene was busy twisting the 5-year-old wedding ring on her finger. With every passing minute, she thought the thin corrosive metal felt like a crown of thorns around her neck. One of her attorneys reached over and placed his hand on her shoulder. But Noelene was in a place littered with palm trees, radiant tropical skies, ocean vistas spangled with noontime light, where white sand licked her toes.

"Will the defendant please stand for the reading of the court's verdict?"

Aided by her counsel, Noelene slowly moved the chair away and stood up over the table. It felt good to stand, she thought. This was not the right time. This was not prudent, but how much time had she? So she turned around and took the time to search through an audience of pupils that stared back at her with no real purpose other than to know why. It did not matter what they thought of her. No, it did not, she reassured herself. But she needed to know. Yes, to know, she said to herself. There, in the back, through the last look of frowning disgust, she found him poured straight up. His face, the closed distance of an adjacent planet – Mars – settling in upon its orbit. Suddenly, she was reminded of the many no-shows, so many letters promising... Part of her asked, why did she bother? The remaining part knew the answer.

"Will the jury foreman rise and announce the verdict to the court?"

A small bald-headed man swallowed and stood above his fear.

With her back turned away from the jury, Noelene remained locked on Hennessey's face.

"We the jury, find the defendant, Noelene Brown... GUILTY, of first-degree murder."

Within an instant, the tissue of the courtroom exploded into a flood of conversations, papers flapping, the opening and closing of briefcases, cameras flowing, tears whispering, and people exiting the courtroom.

"Order in the court," Judge Alright yelled.

From the pit of her stomach came a tug, then another. How many times have I died? Noelene slowly exhaled. In her ears, she heard her lawyers whisper something about an appeal, but she wasn't interested in their advice.

"Order in the COURTROOM." On his face capillaries flared, as his gavel slammed hard on the resilient wood.

"I said ORDER, or I will hold this entire courtroom in contempt!"

Suddenly, the ruckus died.

"Noelene Brown, you have been duly tried by a jury of your peers and found guilty of first-degree murder."

Someone in the audience started crying.

"For the record, do you wish to make a statement?"

Winston, her leading attorney, quickly shot to her ear. She listened, motionless, expressionless, still fiddling with the metallic thorns on her finger.

Noelene nodded.

"Your honor, my client has agreed to a motion for an immediate appeal. Additionally, my client wishes to waive her right to speak before the court."

"Very well, motion accepted and duly recorded."

"As to the matter regarding a possible death penalty, we also wish to enter a plea relative to the obvious nature of her physical condition," Winston continued.

"I am quite aware of your client's physical condition, counselor. Mrs. Brown," Judge Alright continued. "Mrs. Brown!"

"Huh?" Noelene responded.

"How far along are you in your pregnancy?" he continued. "Your pregnancy... Mrs. Brown. When are you due to deliver?"

"I am in my eighth month, your honor."

"Let the court reflect the aforementioned motions and plea."

"Additionally, Mrs. Brown, I think you should know we are scheduling your sentencing hearing immediately following the delivery of your child.

"Please be aware of this fact, as I'm certain your counsel has informed you, because of the nature of your crime, regardless of whether or not you receive the death penalty or life, in accordance with the Federal Regulations surrounding capital punishment, you are subject to lose not only your constitutional rights and privileges, but also all of your maternal obligations to your unborn child.

"In other words, immediately following the birth of your child, your nursing rights and privileges will be revoked, and the court will take into custody your child and rule on an appropriate course of adoptive procedures. Do I make myself clear?"

"Yes... yes, your honor."

Although she had long since prepared herself for this moment, the long hours suckled from the void of a cell, an abortive prison, a hell full of unrelenting psychoses, nipple hatred, despite all of this, she still needed to know. She always knew it was not the best of advice. And she always knew she shouldn't have, but when had she ever listened to good advice? She was still a woman, a woman in love with the backside of Cupid's arrow. So she turned around to discover Hennessey was gone.

"Shall we go, Mrs. Brown?" the female security bailiff asked, jiggling her handcuffs.

"Please, wait..."

Noelene looked up.

A few of the young women whispered, wanting to know who he was.

Noelene stood as if she were in a fog.

With a commanding air that took to the softness of the carpet like an angel commanding clouds, Dr. Peter Matos approached her. He didn't have his usual smile, never really gave one in normal moments, but his tall, tanned, Puerto Rican look was all that was needed to garner gawks and stares from the masses, particularly the female half. His face was shaved smooth, his hair short and peppered with light temporal greying. In the past, Dr. Matos was forever that diamond to which no rough ever knew. In his company, she was always comfortable, safe. He never gave her any reason to fear. Always to her, he was a perfect person.

"Excuse me sir, but you're...," the female bailiff said, challenging Dr. Matos with her authority, pointing at him as he approached, arm raised, hand extended to push him away, "you're not allowed..."

Like a ballroom dancer, he shifted his weight. The power from her forcefulness, her shouldered weight from her rigid insecurity, took her well past his advance. Dr. Matos sidestepped her. He had not touched her, hadn't really paid her any attention. He simply moved away from her attempts and continued on towards Noelene.

Noelene looked up. Her eyes smiled.

"I brought this for you," Dr. Matos said.

"Were you here the whole time?"

"Yes, how could I not?"

"I'm so sorry..."

"Don't say it."

"But..."

"It's okay," he assured her.

Noelene tried to smile.

"Everything is going to turn out just fine."

"It's so nice to see you, Peter."

"Okay, I didn't appreciate...," the bailiff gasped as she picked herself up from the carpet.

"It's okay, ma'am, he's family," Winston interceded.

Grumbling, the bailiff stood with her eyes locked in blackness.

"Thank you, Winston," Peter said.

"No problem. It's good to see you, again."

He and Peter shook hands. The other attorneys did likewise. Dr. Matos took a moment to diagnose her silently, comprehensively.

"Will you do me a favor?" he said.

"I will try... my best."

"Will you try to remember what we've talked about?"

"Do you mean practice?"

"Precisely..."

With head lowered, she thought about time.

"Yes, I promise."

He nodded, approvingly.

"Did you see him?"

He sighed.

"Yes, I saw him. We didn't speak."

Slowly, she shook her head. "I'm not surprised."

"When will you begin to think about yourself?"

"Think about me?" She gazed into the song of brilliance, as if her mind was imbibing Beethoven's *Moonlight Sonata*.

"I know you will do just fine."

"Thank you for coming."

"You know I will be there for you..."

"I know."

Like a bucket in a heavy rainstorm, she collected every second.

"If there's anything I can..."

"No, you've done enough. I am more than grateful."

Noelene turned away.

Dr. Matos looked at Winston.

For a moment, everyone seemed to bathe in the noise of the crowd.

She returned to him.

"This is a present from my collection. I want you to have it."

Noelene held the book in her hands, looked at its name – *I Ch'ing, Book of Changes* – and opened it.

"...this is one of your prized possessions," she said, holding back the tears.

"Yes, it is."

"I know...but..."

"Please take it."

"Thank you."

She reached over, pulled him close, wanting to take him into her, carry his strength, his mystery, erase time. The hug was communication enough. Dr. Matos took his right index finger, touched the tip of her nose with it, and then tapped the same finger to his, twice. She smiled. Afterwards, he turned and walked away.

On his way down the aisle, he gave the bailiff a nod.

While staring into the round, yellowish eyes of the bailiff, Noelene squeezed her wedding band from around her ring finger. Then, she looked at it one last time. In her hand, the ring's weight seemed heavy, glacial.

"Shall we go, Mrs. Brown?" the bailiff asked.

In the center of the long brown table, Noelene planted her wedding band, and was escorted away.

Lost to Follow-up

I went to the woods because I wished to live deliberately, to front only the
essential facts of life, and see if I could not learn what it had to teach, and
not, when I came to die, discover that I had not lived.

> — Henry David Thoreau, *Walden* (1854)

My boss & his boss   needed to speak with me

something about   my rage disrupting office culture

I didn't mind   telling them to shove this job

Went to the bar with a couple of friends

I didn't mind   when the fighting began

I didn't mind the blood   losing old friendships

I began to mind   when the divorce papers arrived

something about   my volatile nightmares

        4am   standing in the middle of my bed

        dripping wet

        knees   arms   torso locked

        heart throbbing at the back of my throat

        yelling 'Eagle down!   Get back!   Medic...!'

        my wife cringing

I remember nothing   just the migraines

Walter Reed Army therapist said

something about   taking pills for PTSD

Medication…!   Hell no!

I am a member of the 47th Airborne

      served two tours in Operation Iraqi Freedom

      thrice in Operation Enduring Freedom

      dodged RPGs   IEDs   stood Green Zone watch

        We don't surrender

        We don't leave anyone behind

        We come home

My home   crashed to the ground   left behind

cars backfiring   are not   my friend

every 4th of July   New Year's Eve

New York City   out of the question

do not sneak up on me   do not

Forests & Parks make the best therapists

      silk conjure   of a free-flowing stream

      pine & oak   perfume the brain

      phloem   xylem aria

      to soothe the shambled self

There

amid Mother Nature   imbibing Æolian songs

I wander

hoping to place my nest   back into the tree

Bitcoin Boulevard

I

Outside Studio 1-A   strolling under three layers of Moulin
    Rouge

a Tamil looking boy   clicked his forty-five heels

    & perfumed the *Fountain of Four Rivers*

    with little red station wagons

    a daisy   short of Duke

An apprentice lover   not quite ready for the tumors of a degree

    paints the water-hard district yellow

    inhales the Green   never forgetting

    to swallow the blue

Walking garden-boulevard   blossoming allusions

    confusions   intrusions the best protrusions

    a flock of spandex angst   living the lust of balls

    pearl-hard jewels   sheered from sheep dogs

    embellished   origins & insertions

Perhaps a writer in the making   he watches colloidal tribes

    page luminous   Isle of Circe

    paragraphs   to thumb to tongue

II

Under mist of hose   lace to pose   his tongue craves for a walk

      along the master blacksmith's   white-hot anvil

Against insolate flames   Szechwan thongs   he beamed the Borg

     From one part of the collective to another

Espousing the prime directive   'Your ass will be immolated'

III

His life a Matisse palette   Petunia   Rhododendron   Wisteria

Ipsilateral ornaments   trembling on the bowstring of Fauves

     pimpled with   *Le bonheur de vivre*

Smacking cheeks hard   against Peter Pan bone

Whenever Ulysses   comes

Everywhere timbre approaching   promising nice
Water lilies voicing wanton vice
Grippingly said with verve & spice
Dante's dance for a world boiling wild rice

IV

Rising like Hazel   the Lady of the Lake   when everyone

pours Starbucks asking why   he returns to

Spin-dry the subterfuge   with Downy Fabric Softener
Vacuum cornered pansies
Wipe the scythe of stiffened hairs

Perhaps he is a writer   Off the Wall

V

Revived by sirens   skirting cornered violins   silly putty awakens

    already handled   already shaped

    as bow ribbons tightened   with a disturbing pith

Birds sing from solstice to equinox

They sing before the dawn   they string just after sunset

They sing beyond   exotic lips of the purple strip

    up   out   to quench the night

Whispering from   Ritz Carlton suites   skyscraper penthouses

whispering everywhere   Et in Arcadia Ego

Forever in passage   forever untenable   daises blow
Shifting under sonnet storms of an untoward you
Penetrating voices   maternally lectured to

Come daisy   close the box gnawing at lessons of un-love   upright like

    five-thousand-year old Stonehenge breasts

Come   Let us light your broken cigarette under the streetlamp

    of your denouement   your corpus   your wreathing plot

Come Hermes   stand amongst our accordion hedges of lilac pixels

    laced   as one last   short drag

Varicose Rain

Hovering water   slices lighthouse
born of swan   shuffles away
like drizzle   wiggling ill

Against shoreline valences
against tense calcarine space
        I smell warm Quaker Oats
        I smell my ancestor's calendar bones
cello swirling
sweet marrow rememberings —
        Pink flamingo   celosia butterfly dew   strung soft
           along wings of a velvet Aurora
        pace wafting   in the ankle flight
           of Hermes on the rocks
        taste flung weather-sweet
           like a galaxy-hung instance
        tercets webbed   with wisdom-spun threads
           only a fly would lay warm against

Perhaps   a quotient of ticks   indivisible tocks
sketched from a sinuous silence

Perhaps   a soup   of self-stares back
through someone else
        long since   given
        long since   forgotten

Blue Oyster Toes

This osmotic smile

wrinkles   faceless strains

I watch long horizons

serve orchestral winds   assembled full

I hear another day

quietly huddled   beautifully played

Around blue oyster toes

moon beans lacerate viscous wills

            shells chime

Placid desires   swing across alligator sand

I   dance untasted

      habitats reflect

enjoy wet leaves gathering beneath earth's hem

still against the residue of bustling quasars

       olfactory senses parade

while harp strings

compose another pearl

fulfilling   as a glass of mother's warm milk

Within this lyrical lithe

tides lick Noah's park

I linger under   this buoyant skirt of heaven

        this wet returning bassinette

basking sustenance

basking grace

        this maternal place of

I listen to   splendor

flows   with purpose

Collateral Wind
Arrested as Mill

Always on the prowl   it began as a whisper

A moment motioning   with whip-o-will sheen

A soulful broth   fallen from a shy cherub

      between acetaminophen streets

      intracranial stalls   a den of lotteries

      autistic walls

Can you hear it?

That audience blinking sand

Sibilant chatter beneath a flame   running centigrade wax

      seeking shape hue coolness of a silent state

      fixed. A place free from choreography —

      Balanchine   Kelly   Nureyev

      words & music by Rogers & Hammerstein

At the gate of Then   he bends his horse stance into cedar lane

Dahlia pain   Stalking the timelessness of Oklahoma

germinating as a botanical garden

In the end   wind always gives way

Never dies   waits for the next breath   the next whisper

      and then   another

      where he   inhales the silence of a screeching dream

      wound as windmill   listening

Listening to Night

Light of day is pyramid —
With hieroglyphic heat   erased
the atmosphere palpates   naked throbs
a blanket of lambent beauty   synaptic thrums.
Under Pleiades whispering breezes forested wimples
Pan giggled when I tripped over branched veins.

Pillow without light is bliss —
cypress murmurs to the sway of mews tracking summer nymphs.
Behind Helios armor-piercing thumbs press bones down
surfing across Jordan on civilized rafts. Before evergreen
before crackling dew swells & swirls & swishes
pugilistic kisses perennial willow in the lean.

Beneath Iris a symphony plays mute
& I drink scents of Psyche & Eros
Amber-blue flames courtship along a hushed stream.
There you are fetal against the milk tongue.

There, —
  among lectures of a professorial night
  among skirting aromas of birch & maple & pine & redwood
  among acorns & chestnuts & maidenhair fern
  among bridal suites of hypanthium
  among this natural classroom shining Ithaca
I listen to night

Occipital Train Ride

Above the brazen dawn, clouds ride the early morning dark blue sky, approaching quietude. Its peaceful enrolment seems endless, the meditation of vastness and existence raining a truth I hear as a universal Song of Songs, the holiest of holy that makes my queries regarding need, everything surrounding *self* – irrelevant. Against the public cloth, I sit like a pea in a pod, listening to the rollicking train as it hugs the tracks, shaking intentions fueled by schedules, cell phones, halitosis, a sermon of eyes, and frolicking agendas. There, I view the pulpit of the universe, listening to the hymn of heavenly bodies churn and squeak, slowly grind their mathematical equations against the gravitational forces of desire, personal truth, contemplating why we remain forever hungry for another morsel of time.

This is a moment when knowledge about the name of the day drops far and away from memory, when the hands of time lay wasted with the diagnosis of Carpal Tunnel syndrome. Whenever I fall into this *meditative state*, I invariably feel as if I'm tasting milk and honey for the first time, maybe having my first kiss... Odd, it all seems, to dream in top-shelf memories, to walk through an existence subsisting on an Olympic decathlon.

Within a blink of an eye, another drink of breath, the early morning sky rushes in with an illuminated flat, whitewashing of clouds that glide like unfinished neonatal dreams, hovering afterthoughts discussing the poetry of a new day, perhaps another stanza, speaking to the afterbirth of a blessed existence.

Serenity

A leaf. Nature's DNA. Ephemeral fragments of a seasonal, civilized (primitive) world. Arranged in alphabetical order as an evanescent experience. Wrapped within a glass of communion elegantly poured. Winter prospering spring. Extracted blue. Deliberately. Lawfully.

Who doesn't long for high places? Wandering in translucent unity along the credenza of a splendid sky. Fine free fog flowing. Arresting in pointing cognizance. With a blanket of mother's whiskers, beard, blossoming below. And values drifting like hosts through waterfall songs. Singing Walden notes, orchestrated from a heavenly source.

From rustling leaves, comes a cello. From the spider's web, a violin. From a soaring flock of geese, comes a harp. From the great open, a symphony. And from this, could you have danced all night? From all of this, the sense of red and blue and green and yellow and brown; subliminal lakes of rainbows. Majesty. An absorbed quest driven to the limit of creativity; imagination suffused as an enunciation. Embrace the simple dignity of purity, the moods of light, pulling up pants of a miraculous future.

Through the heavy sweetness of a glorious nature, a host of angels whisper in grace.

Poetry Acknowledgments

1. "Amygdala Blue," *Ars Medica, A Journal of Medicine, the Arts, and Humanities*, Vol. 4 (1), Fall 2007, p. 103-104

2. "The Blood of Rain", *Wrath-Bearing Tree*, January 2020

3. "Durn My Hide", *Blue Mountain Review*, 304 (2), Spring 2020; p. 44

4. "Panther Lurking High above the Hood," *Making/Connections – Interdisciplinary Approaches to Cultural Diversity Journal*, Vol. 12, No. 1 (September 2010) pp. 40-40. Doi: 10.5555/maco.12.1.7r4345025285mm28

5. "Silent as Impression Made by Stone", *Wrath-Bearing Tree*, January 2020

6. "Sown Dry", *Blue Mountain Review*, 49 (3), Spring 2020; p. 278

7. "Hippocampal Lash", *African American Review*, 49 (3), Fall 2016; p. 278. Doi: 10.1353/afa.2016.0039

8. "Sir, Yes Sir", *Wrath-Bearing Tree*, January 2020

9. "Furious Flowers," *Jelly Bucket*, Issue #11, 2021, p. 112

10. "Bitcoin Boulevard", (Originally published as "Engaging Screensavers," *Pank Magazine*, 5 (10), October 2010

11. "Blue Oyster Toes", *Blue Mountain Review*, 49 (3), Spring 2020; p. 278

12. "Listening to Night", *North American Review*, 304 (2), Spring 2019; p. 44. (ISSN:0029-2397)

About Atmosphere Press

Atmosphere Press is an independent, full-service publisher for excellent books in all genres and for all audiences. Learn more about what we do at atmospherepress.com.

We encourage you to check out some of Atmosphere's latest releases, which are available at Amazon.com and via order from your local bookstore:

Until the Kingdom Comes, poetry by Jeanne Lutz

Warcrimes, poetry by GOODW.Y.N

The Freedom of Lavenders, poetry by August Reynolds

Convalesce, poetry by Enne Zale

Poems for the Bee Charmer (And Other Familiar Ghosts), poetry by Jordan Lentz

Serial Love: When Happily Ever After... Isn't, poetry by Kathy Kay

Flowers That Die, poetry by Gideon Halpin

Through The Soul Into Life, poetry by Shoushan B

Embrace The Passion In A Lover's Dream, poetry by Paul Turay

Reflections in the Time of Trumpius Maximus, poetry by Mark Fishbein

Drifters, poetry by Stuart Silverman

As a Patient Thinks about the Desert, poetry by Rick Anthony Furtak

Winter Solstice, poetry by Diana Howard

Blindfolds, Bruises, and Break-Ups, poetry by Jen Schneider

Songs of Snow and Silence, poetry by Jen Emery

INHABITANT, poetry by Charles Crittenden

Godless Grace, poetry by Michael Terence O'Brien

March of the Mindless, poetry by Thomas Walrod

In the Village That Is Not Burning Down, poetry by Travis Nathan Brown

About the Author

Paul Lomax worked formerly as Quality Assurance Scientist and Acting Director with the US Army. He earned his EdD in Education Psychology from Duquesne University. He is a graduate of the University of Pennsylvania MLA program, where he studied African-American Literature and Psychology. He has poetry published in *Jelly Bucket, Blue Mountain Review, North American Review, African American Review, Wrath-Bearing Tree, PANK, Making/Connections – Interdisciplinary Approaches to Cultural Diversity, Ars Medica – A Journal of Medicine, the Arts, and the Humanities*. In his free time, he enjoys Chess (5-minute quick), Cryptocurrency investing, psychosocial politics and luxurious Irish Single Malt Whiskey.

www.ingramcontent.com/pod-product-compliance
Lightning Source LLC
Chambersburg PA
CBHW031348060726
47590CB00007B/2674